Six Wagnerian sopranos

Leider : Flagstad : Varnay
Mödl : Nilsson : Jones

Discographies compiled by
John Hunt

1994

Wagnerian Sopranos
Published by John Hunt.
Designed by Richard Chluparty
© 1994 John Hunt
reprinted 2009
ISBN 978-0-951026-89-2

Sole distributors:
Travis & Emery,
17 Cecil Court,
London, WC2N 4EZ,
United Kingdom.
(+44) 20 7 459 2129.
sales@travis-and-emery.com

Acknowledgement

This publication has been made possible by generous support from the following:

Richard Ames, New Barnet
Yoshihiro Asada, Osaka
Jonathan Brown, Paris
Roger Brown, London
Guy Burkill, London
Edward Chibas, Caracas
John Derry, Newcastle-upon-Tyne
K. Eayrs, Alderley Edge
Henry Fogel, Chicago
Peter Fulop, Toronto
J.-P. Goossens, Luxembourg
Peter Hamann, Bochum
Tadashi Hasegawa, Nagoya
Martin Hickley, Godalming
Martin Holland, Sale
John Hughes, Brisbane
Michael Jones, Birmingham
Eric Kobe, Lucerne
John Larsen, Mariager
Ernst Lumpe, Soest
John Meriton, Manchester
Gregory Page-Turner, Bridport
Tully Potter, Billericay
D. Priddon, London
Gordon Reeves, Birmingham
Robin Scott, Bradford
Clare Shepherd, Beckenham
R. Simmons, Brentford
Kazuhiko Soma, Kawasaki
Neville Sumpter, Northolt
Carl Suneson, Stockholm
Yoshihiko Suzuki, Tokyo
Malcolm Walker, Harrow
Björn Westberg, Saltsjö-Boo

Contents

3	Acknowledgement
5	Introduction
7	Frida Leider
35	Kirsten Flagstad
121	Astrid Varnay
161	Martha Mödl
185	Birgit Nilsson
247	Gwyneth Jones
285	Credits

Published 1994 by John Hunt

Designed by Richard Chlupaty, London

Copyright 1994   John Hunt

Six Wagnerian sopranos

Such has been the power of Wagner's music in the 150 years or so since it was conceived, as much on performers as on listeners, that many generations of singers have been active whose main careers were devoted to interpreting the oeuvre of the Bayreuth master.

The purpose of these discographies, however, is to place the Wagner work of the chosen sopranos in the broader context of their recording careers in general. There have indeed been few Wagner specialists who have not appreciated the value of other composers' music in keeping their voices supple, although Wagnerian stamina has not necessarily been a pre-requisite, for example, in performing Mozart. The main Mozart operatic role which seems to have interested Wagnerian sopranos after Lilli Lehmann has been Donna Anna in Don Giovanni, but their success in playing it has been variable.

Piecemeal as it may seem by modern standards, the recorded output of the earliest of our sopranos, Frida Leider, is remarkably comprehensive in illustrating her versatility both in and outside the Wagner area (it is also conveniently available in its virtual entirety on a series of compact discs produced by the Austrian company Preiser). Leider remains, not without good reason, the modern Wagner soprano of the 20th century, and not just in the memories of those who heard her in Berlin, Bayreuth, Covent Garden, Milan or San Francisco.

Only a singer like Kirsten Flagstad, whose career survived the traumas of World War II (and her authorised biography, The Flagstad Manuscript by Louis Biancolli, shows how it almost did not), came to benefit from the enormous strides made in recording techniques and the dissemination of recordings between the 1920s and 1950s. Flagstad was able, by dint of her impeccable and well-schooled technique, to launch herself into a second (LP) recording career at an age when most of her generation were contemplating retirement.

Yet many Metropolitan Opera broadcasts had already captured Flagstad in complete roles even before the LP format had been perfected. Most of these were of course issued unofficially, some not at all, but in view of the wide availability of unauthorised broadcasts and the publicity given to them in recent books like Saturday Afternoons at the Met, I have decided to include at least a mention of them in these discographies.

Indeed, in the case of the post-war singers, 3 out of 4 of those dealt with did not really capture the imaginations of commercial recording companies, and we are therefore reliant on a wealth of live material to round out the sound pictures of Varnay, Mödl and Jones.

Video material may well provide future generations of collectors with valuable insight into stage performance styles, therefore I have included selected video items in the discographies even if they are as yet inaccessible on a commercial basis. The possibility of mass-produced videos similar to "pirate" LPs and CDs remains a thing of the future.

As far as the song repertory is concerned, I have decided to facilitate the reader's search for individual songs by listing them under their separate titles even when they form part of a cycle or sequence (it should also be borne in mind that actual titles of songs sometimes differ from the words of their first lines).

A list of those who have generously helped me with research and data appears elsewhere, but I have to single out my friend Clifford Elkin, whom I have subjected to endless lists of questions about the contents of records which I do not possess. His patience with my not always logical questioning has been infinite !

John Hunt

Frida Leider
1888-1975

Discography compiled by John Hunt

Introduction

One day I received from His Master's Voice an invitation to sing the opening scene of the second act of Die Walküre with Friedrich Schorr under the direction of Leo Blech. The recording was fixed for one o'clock in the Berlin Singakademie with the orchestra of the Staatsoper. I can still recall the stage fright that seized me before this recording. It is much easier to sing Brünnhilde's battle-cry in costume and make-up, and in action on the stage; it is quite another thing to sing it before the microphone in the middle of the day, keeping quite still.

Early in the morning I began to sing myself in, and had prepared myself thoroughly before driving to the Singakademie at 12 o'clock; there, too, I continued to warm my voice in the artists' room. My colleague Schorr and I exchanged no words; he too found himself in a similarly excited state.

Suddenly I heard at a distance the splendid music that introduces the second act. I slowly approached the desk and watched Leo Blech; I was almost certain that he too saw me, but he revealed nothing. His method was always the right one to restore a singer's confidence. Later he greeted us briefly, and remained quite calm and practical, as at a stage rehearsal. The recording engineers had all arrived and asked us for a trial run-through. But, thanks to the gifted and sympathetic conducting of Leo Blech, the trial run was so successful that it proved possible to use it for the final record. So far as I know, this is the only time such a thing has ever happened in recording this scene.

The Brünnhilde of Götterdämmerung was certainly one of my favourite roles. But there was hardly a single performance at which I did not feel nervous in the final scene, in which my horse, Grane, almost always sprung some new surprise on me. I seldom had a quiet horse; it is understanable that animals in an entirely unfamiliar atmosphere, filled with singing and orchestral sound, should become extremely nervous.

My worst experience was during a performance at La Scala Milan, when Grane accompanied my final scene with unbroken pawing of the right foreleg. He wanted sugar, as his attendant had told me behind the scenes. But even the sugar that I always had in readiness could do nothing to quieten his capers. Other Granes would pull at the bridle and tear my arm aloft, or nibble at my wig; they would begin to frisk; even to snort. In such situations it was hard to preserve my calm and to concentrate.

Finally, I pleaded energetically that a horse should no longer be allowed to appear in Brünnhilde's final scene, since, in my opinion, live animals have no place on the operatic stage. In spite of strong opposition, I carried my point, and thenceforward horses have been banished during the finale of Götterdämmerung.

Frida Leider 1959

Royal Opera Covent Garden

LONDON & PROVINCIAL OPERA SOCIETY SEASON
Artistic Director: Sir Thomas Beecham, Bart.
Secretary & Manager: Charles A. Barrand

Der Ring des Nibelungen
RICHARD WAGNER

Monday, May 17th, 1937, at 5.45
In German

DIE WALKÜRE

Siegmund	FRANZ VÖLKER
Hunding	LUDWIG WEBER
Wotan	RUDOLF BOCKELMANN
Sieglinde	MARIA MÜLLER
Brünnhilde	FRIDA LEIDER
Fricka	MARGARETE KLOSE
Gerhilde	MAE CRAVEN
Ortlinde	THELMA BARDSLEY
Waltraute	LINDA SEYMOUR
Schwertleite	GLADYS RIPLEY
Helmwige	ELSA STENNING
Siegrune	EDITH COATES
Grimgerde	GWLADYS GARSIDE
Rossweisse	EVELYN ARDEN

Conductor . Dr. WILHELM FURTWÄNGLER

Beethoven

Ah perfido!

Berlin 1922	Orchestra Unnamed conductor	78: Polydor 65745 LP: Scala (USA) 835 LP: Preiser LV 240 CD: Preiser 89301

Fidelio: Excerpt (Abscheulicher, wo eilst du hin?)

Berlin 1921	Orchestra Unnamed conductor	78: Polydor 65743 LP: Preiser LV 240 CD: Preiser 89301
London May 1928	Orchestra Barbirolli	78: HMV D 1497 78: Electrola EJ 338 78: Victor 7118 45: Electrola 7EGW 8471/ E 40156 LP: HMV COLH 132 LP: Electrola WCLP 799/E 83386 LP: Preiser LV 30 LP: Historia H 644 LP: EMI 1C 147 30785-30786M CD: Preiser 89004

Leider 11

Gluck

<u>Alceste: Excerpt (Divinités du Styx)</u>

Berlin   Orchestra   Unpublished German Radio
December 1933   Unnamed conductor   recording RRG 212.1703-1704
                 <u>Sung in German</u>

<u>Armide: Excerpt (Ah, si la liberté)</u>

London   Orchestra   78: HMV D 1547
May 1928   Barbirolli   78: Electrola EJ 339
                                        45: Electrola 7EGW 8471/E 40156
                                        LP: HMV COLH 132
                                        LP: Preiser LV 30
                                        LP: EMI 1C 147 30785-30786M
                                        CD: Preiser 89004

Mozart

Don Giovanni: Excerpt (Or sai chi l'onore)

Berlin 1925	Orchestra Unnamed conductor Sung in German	78: Polydor 72976 LP: Eterna (USA) 477/745 LP: Scala (USA) 835 LP: Preiser LV 172 CD: Preiser 89301
London May 1928	Orchestra Barbirolli	78: HMV D 1547 78: Electrola EJ 339 LP: HMV COLH 132/CSLP 503 LP: Electrola E 83886 LP: Preiser LV 30 LP: Top Artists Platter T 318 LP: EMI 1C 14/ 30785-30786M LP: EMI EX 29 05983 CD: Preiser 89004 CD: EMI CMS 763 7502

Le Nozze di Figaro: Excerpt (Dove sono)

Berlin 1921	Orchestra Unnamed conductor Sung in German	78: Polydor 65744 LP: Scala (USA) 835 CD: Preiser 89301

Le Nozze di Figaro: Excerpt (Porgi amor)

Berlin 1921	Orchestra Unnamed conductor Sung in German	78: Polydor 65744 LP: Preiser LV 240 CD: Preiser 89301 Later pressings of the 78 version substituted the 1925 recording listed below
Berlin 1925	Orchestra Unnamed conductor Sung in German	78: Polydor 65744 LP: Scala (USA) 835 LP: Preiser LV 172 CD: Preiser 89301

Puccini

Tosca: Excerpts (Ah! quegli occhi; Amaro sol perte)

Berlin 1922	Günther Orchestra Unnamed conductor Sung in German	78: Polydor 65687 LP: Preiser LV 177 CD: Preiser 89301

Tosca: Excerpt (Vissi d'arte)

Berlin 1921	Orchestra Unnamed conductor Sung in German	78: Polydor 72835/72875 LP: Preiser LV 240 CD: Preiser 89301

Schubert

Auf dem Wasser zu singen

Berlin January 1941	Raucheisen, piano	78: Electrola DB 5625 LP: Electrola WCLP 799/E 83386 LP: Preiser LV 145 LP: EMI 1C 147 30785-30786M LP: EMI RLS 766 RLS 766 incorrectly dated November 1943

Erlkönig

Berlin January 1941	Raucheisen, piano	78: Electrola DB 5625 LP: Preiser LV 145 LP: EMI 1C 147 30785-30786M

Frühlingstraum (Winterreise)

Berlin January 1942	Raucheisen, piano	LP: Electrola WCLP 799/E 83386 LP: Preiser LV 145 LP: EMI 1C 147 30785-30786M Also issued by the singer herself on a private acetate with a spoken greeting to her English friends

Schumann

Die Blume der Ergebung

Berlin Raucheisen, piano LP: Preiser LV 145
1944

Du nennst mich armes Mädchen

Berlin Raucheisen, piano LP: Preiser LV 145
1944

Einsamkeit

Berlin Raucheisen, piano LP: Preiser LV 145
1944

Erstes Grün

Berlin Raucheisen, piano LP: Preiser LV 145
1944

Die Fensterscheibe

Berlin Raucheisen, piano LP: Preiser LV 145
1944

Marienwürmchen

Berlin Raucheisen, piano 78: Electrola DB 5626
January 1941   LP: Electrola WCLP 799/E 83386
                                     LP: Preiser LV 145
                                     LP: EMI 1C 147 30705-30786M

Meine Rose

Berlin   Raucheisen, piano   78: Electrola DB 5626
January 1941   LP: Electrola WCLP 799/E 83386
                                             LP: Preiser LV 145
                                             LP: Rubini CC 2
                                             LP: EMI 1C 147 30785-30786M
                                             LP: EMI RLS 154 7003
                                             <u>RLS 154 7003 incorrectly states</u>
                                             <u>recording made November 1943</u>

Mond, du meiner Seele Liebling

Berlin   Raucheisen, piano   LP: Preiser LV 145
1944

Der Nussbaum (Myrthen)

Berlin   Raucheisen, piano   LP: Electrola WCLP 799/E 83386
January 1942   LP: Preiser LV 145
                                             LP: EMI 1C 147 30785-30786M
                                             <u>Also issued by the singer</u>
                                             <u>herself on a private acetate</u>
                                             <u>with a spoken greeting to</u>
                                             <u>her English friends</u>

Singet nicht in Trauertönen

Berlin   Raucheisen, piano   LP: Preiser LV 145
1944

Viel Glück zur Reise, Schwalben

Berlin   Raucheisen, piano   LP: Preiser LV 145
1944

Widmung (Myrthen)

Berlin   Raucheisen, piano   78: Electrola DB 5626
January 1941   LP: Electrola WCLP 799/E 83386
                                             LP: Preiser LV 145
                                             LP: EMI 1C 147 30785-30786M
                                             LP: EMI RLS 154 7003
                                             <u>RLS 154 7003 incorrectly states</u>
                                             <u>recording made November 1943</u>

16 Leider

Richard Strauss

<u>Ariadne auf Naxos: Excerpt (Es gibt ein Reich)</u>

Berlin   Orchestra   78: Polydor 72976
1925   Unnamed conductor   LP: Preiser LV 172
                                      CD: Preiser 89301

Verdi

Aida: Excerpt (Ritorna vincitor)

Berlin	Orchestra	78: Polydor 65641
1922	Unnamed conductor	LP: Preiser LV 240
	<u>Sung in German</u>	LP: Rococo 5241
		CD: Preiser 89301

Aida: Excerpt (O patria mia)

Berlin	Orchestra	78: Polydor 65641
1921	Unnamed conductor	LP: Preiser LV 240
	<u>Sung in German</u>	LP: Rococo 5241
		CD: Preiser 89301

Aida: Excerpts (Pur ti riveggo; Fuggiam gli ardor)

Berlin	Günther	78: Polydor 65691
1922	Orchestra	LP: Preiser LV 177
	Unnamed conductor	LP: Rococo 5241
	<u>Sung in German</u>	CD: Preiser 89301

Un Ballo in maschera: Excerpt (Ve' se di notte)

Berlin 1925	Helgers, Abendroth, Schlusnus Orchestra Unnamed conductor Sung in German	78: Polydor 72961 LP: Preiser LV 155 LP: Rococo 5241 CD: Preiser 89301

Don Carlo: Excerpt (O don fatale)

Berlin 1926	Orchestra Unnamed conductor	78: Polydor 72998 LP: Scala (USA) 835 LP: Rococo 5241 LP: Preiser LV 172 CD: Preiser 89301
Berlin 1927	Orchestra Unnamed conductor	Polydor unpublished

Il Trovatore: Excerpt (Tacea la notte placida)

Berlin 1926	Orchestra Unnamed conductor Sung in German	78: Polydor 72975 LP: Preiser LV 155 LP: Rococo 5241 CD: Preiser 89301

Il Trovatore: Excerpt (D'amor sull'ali rosee)

Berlin 1925	Orchestra Unnamed conductor Sung in German	78: Polydor 72975 LP: Preiser LV 155 LP: Rococo 5241 CD: Preiser 89301

Il Trovatore: Excerpt (Di geloso amor)

Berlin 1925	Hutt, Schlusnus Orchestra Unnamed conductor Sung in German	78: Polydor 72961 LP: Preiser LV 155 LP: Rococo 5241 CD: Preiser 89301

Il Trovatore: Excerpts (Mira d'acerbe lagrima: Vivra! Contente il giubilo)

Berlin 1925	Schlusnus Orchestra Unnamed conductor Sung in German	78: Polydor 72988 LP: Eterna (USA) 477/745 LP: Rococo 5241 LP: Preiser LV 155 CD: Preiser 89301

Leider 19

Wagner

Der fliegende Holländer: Excerpt (Traft ihr das Schiff)

Berlin	Orchestra	78: Polydor 72978
1925	Unnamed conductor	LP: Scala (USA) 835
		LP: Rococo 5228
		LP: Eterna 820 795
		LP: Preiser LV 172
		CD: Preiser 89301

Der fliegende Holländer: Excerpt (Fühlst du den Schmerz)

Berlin	Günther	78: Polydor 65704
1922	Orchestra	LP: Rococo 5228
	Unnamed conductor	LP: Eterna 820 795
		LP: Preiser LV 177
		CD: Preiser 89301

Götterdämmerung: Excerpt (Zu neuen Taten)

Berlin   Soot   78: Polydor 72984
1925   Orchestra   LP: Preiser LV 155
    Unnamed conductor   CD: Preiser 89301
        CD: Legato LCD 146
<u>Only as far as Brünnhilde brennt dann ewig dir in der Brust</u>:
LP: Rococo 5228
LP: Eterna 820 795

20   Leider

Götterdämmerung, Act 1:Excerpts (Wär' wider mich Wotans Sinn erweicht?-
Höre mit Sinn, was ich dir sage!-Brünnhild'! Ein Freier kam)

London May 1936	Thorborg, Melchior LPO Beecham	Columbia/HMV unpublished test pressings LP: Ed Smith EJS 167/UORC 234 CD: Legato LCD 146

Götterdämmerung, Act 2: Excerpts (Brünnhild', die hehrste Frau-Helle
Wehr! Heilige Waffe!-Welches Unholds List)

London May 1936	Nezadal, Melchior, Janssen, Weber LPO Covent Garden Chorus Beecham	LP: Ed Smith EJS 167/UORC 234 LP: Acanta 22.863/98.221776 CD: Legato LCD 146 CD: Acanta 44.1055 Ed Smith and Acanta incorrectly name conductor as Furtwängler; entire second act of this performance was supposed to exist as Columbia/HMV test pressings
London June 1938	Stosch, Melchior, Janssen, Schirp LPO Covent Garden Chorus Furtwängler	LP: Ed Smith EJS 342 LP: Acanta 40.23502 CD: Pearl GEMMCD 9331 Acanta extract stops before Welches Unholds List; EJS 342 incorrectly dated July 1938

Götterdämmerung: Excerpt (1.Schweigt eures Jammers; 2.Starke Scheite schichtet
mir dort)

Berlin October (2) and November (1) 1928	Marherr-Wagner (1) Staatskapelle Blech	78: HMV D 2025-2026 78: Electrola EJ 420-421 LP: HMV COLH 105 LP: Electrola E 80665 LP: Eterna (USA) 480 (2 only) LP: Preiser LV 1370 LP: EMI 1C 147 30785-30786M LP: EMI 1C 181 30669-30678M (2 only) LP: EMI RLS 7711 CD: Legato LCD 146 CD: Pearl GEMMCD 9331 Also published on LP by by Discocorp and described as a 1937 Bayreuth performance conducted by Furtwängler

An unpublished Met broadcast of Götterdämmerung may be preserved: according
to Metropolitan Opera Annals a live relay with Leider in the role of Brünnhilde took place on 17 February 1933

Parsifal: Excerpt (Ich sah das Kind)

Berlin 1925	Orchestra Unnamed conductor	78: Polydor 72977 LP: Rococo 5228 LP: Preiser LV 155 LP: Eterna 820 795 LP: DG 2721 115 CD: Preiser 89301
London May 1931	LSO Barbirolli	78: HMV DB 1545 78: Victor 7523 45: Victor 17-0007 LP: Victor LCT 1001 LP: HMV COLH 132 LP: Preiser LV 30 LP: EMI 1C 147 30785-30786M LP: EMI 1C 181 30669-30678M LP: EMI RLS 7711/EX 29 02123 CD: Preiser 89004 CD: EMI CMS 764 0082 CD: Pearl GEMMCD 9331

An unpublished Met broadcast may be preserved: according to Metropolitan Opera Annals a live relay with Leider in the role of Kundry took place on 9 March 1933

Rienzi: Excerpt (Gerechter Gott!)

Berlin 1921	Orchestra Unnamed conductor	78: Polydor 65704 LP: Rococo 5228 LP: Preiser LV 240 LP: Eterna 820 795 CD: Preiser 89301

Siegfried: Excerpt (Closing scene)

For the purposes of acoustic and early electrical recordings, an extended scene such as this was divided into sections of appropriate length :-

Heil dir Sonne! Heil dir Licht!

Berlin 1925	Soot Orchestra Unnamed conductor	78: Polydor 72985 LP: Scala (USA) 835 LP: Eterna (USA) 477/745 LP: Preiser LV 172 CD: Preiser 89301
Berlin September 1927	Laubenthal Staatskapelle Blech	78: HMV D 1535 78: Electrola EJ 371 78: Victor 9813 LP: Preiser LV 30 LP: Top Artists Platter T 322 LP: EMI 1C 147 30785-30786M LP: EMI EX 29 02123 CD: EMI CMS 764 0082 CD: Preiser 89004

Ewig war ich

Berlin 1925	Orchestra Unnamed conductor	78: Polydor 72977 LP: Rococo 5228 LP: Preiser LV 172 LP: Eterna 820 795 LP: DG 2721 110 CD: Preiser 89301
Berlin September 1927	Staatskapelle Blech	78: HMV D 1532 78: Electrola EJ 370 78: Victor 9814 LP: Preiser LV 30 LP: EMI 1C 147 30785-30786M LP: EMI EX 29 02123 CD: EMI CMS 764 0082 CD: Preiser 89004

O Siegfried! Dein war ich von je

Berlin 1925	Soot Orchestra Unnamed conductor	78: Polydor 72985 LP: Scala (USA) 835 LP: Eterna (USA) 477/745 LP: Preiser LV 172 LP: Top Artists Platter T 322 CD: Preiser 89301 <u>This versions begins at O kindischer Held!</u>
Berlin September 1927	Laubenthal Staatskapelle Blech	78: HMV D 1535 78: Electrola EJ 371 78: Victor 9814 LP: Preiser LV 30 LP: EMI 1C 147 30785-30786M LP: EMI EX 29 02123 CD: EMI CMS 764 0082 CD: Preiser 89004

Siegfried: Excerpt (Closing scene)

Frankfurt August 1934	Lorenz Orchestra Unnamed conductor	Unpublished German Radio recording RRG 20302 & 20315

Tannhäuser: Excerpt (Dich teure Halle)

Berlin 1921	Orchestra Unnamed conductor	78: Polydor 65627 LP: Rococo 5228 LP: Scala (USA) 835 LP: Eterna (USA) 477/745 LP: Preiser LV 240 LP: Eterna 820 795 CD: Preiser 89301
Berlin 1926	Orchestra Unnamed conductor	78: Polydor 73052 LP: Preiser LV 1370 CD: Preiser 89301 <u>78 version may not have been published</u>

Tristan und Isolde, miscellaneous excerpts, many fragmentary

New York March 1933	Olszewska, Melchior, Schorr/Schützendorf, L.Hofmann Metropolitan Orchestra & Chorus Bodansky	LP: Ed Smith EJS 499 <u>Schorr and Schützendorf are</u> <u>both heard in the part of</u> <u>Kurwenal as this is an</u> <u>amalgamation of broadcasts</u> <u>on 3 and 11 March</u>

Tristan und Isolde: Excerpt (Doch nun von Tristan?-Er schwur mit tausend Eiden)

Berlin November 1928	Marherr-Wagner Staatskapelle Blech	78: HMV D 1667 78: Electrola EJ 301 78: Victor 1603 LP: Preiser LV 1370 LP: HMV COLH 132 LP: EMI 1C 147 30785-30786M LP: EMI RLS 7711/EX 29 02123 CD: EMI CMS 764 0082 CD: Pearl GEMMCD 9331 CD: Legato LCD 146 CD: Nimbus NI 7848 Er schwur mit tausend Eiden LP: EMI 1C 181 30669-30678M

Tristan und Isolde: Excerpt (Mild und leise)

Berlin 1921	Orchestra Unnamed conductor	78: Polydor 65627 LP: Scala (USA) 835 LP: Eterna (USA) 477/745 LP: Preiser LV 240 LP: Eterna 820 795 CD: Preiser 89301
London May 1931	LSO Barbirolli	78: HMV DB 1545 78: Victor 7523 LP: HMV COLH 132 LP: Electrola WCLP 799/E 83386 LP: Preiser LV 30 LP: EMI 1C 147 30785-30786M CD: Pearl GEMMCD 9331 CD: Legato LCD 146 CD: Preiser 89004

Tristan und Isolde: Excerpt (Liebesnacht)

For the purposes of acoustic and early electrical recordings, an extended scene such as this was divided into sections of appropriate length :-

Isolde! Geliebte! Tristan! Geliebter!

Berlin 1925	Soot Orchestra Unnamed conductor	LP: Preiser LV 143 CD: Preiser 89301 Extract ends at Ewig, ewig ein
London May 1929	Melchior LSO Coates	HMV unpublished
Berlin September 1929	Melchior Staatskapelle Coates	78: HMV D 1723 78: Electrola EJ 482 78: Victor 7273 LP: HMV COLH 132 LP: Preiser LV 30 LP: Eterna (USA) 480 LP: EMI 1C 147 01259-01260M LP: EMI RLS 7711/EX 29 02123 LP: Danacord DACO 119-120 CD: Danacord DACOCD 315-316 CD: EMI CMS 764 0082 CD: Preiser 89004 CD: Claremont GSE 78-50-26 CD: Music and Arts CD 5026 CD: Legato LCD 146

Doch es rächte sich der verscheuchte Tag

London May 1929	Melchior LSO Coates	HMV unpublished
Berlin September 1929	Melchior Staatskapelle Coates	78: HMV D 1723 78: Electrola EJ 482 78: Victor 7273 LP: HMV COLH 132 LP: EMI 1C 147 01259-01260M LP: Preiser LV 30 LP: EMI RLS 7711/EX 29 02123 LP: Danacord DACO 119-120 CD: Danacord DACOCD 315-316 CD: EMI CMS 764 0082 CD: Preiser 89004 CD: Claremont GSE 78-50-26 CD: Music and Arts CD 5026 CD: Legato LCD 146

Tristan und Isolde: Excerpt (Liebesnacht)/continued

O sink' hernieder, Nacht der Liebe

Berlin 1925	Soot Orchestra Unnamed conductor	LP: Preiser LV 143 CD: Preiser 89301
London May 1929	Melchior LSO Coates	78: HMV D 1724 78: Electrola EJ 483 78: Victor 7274 LP: HMV COLH 132 LP: Electrola WCLP 799/E 83386 LP: Preiser LV 30 LP: EMI 1C 147 01259-01260M LP: EMI RLS 7711/EX 29 02123 LP: Danacord DACO 119-120 CD: Danacord DACOCD 315-316 CD: EMI CMS 764 0082 CD: Preiser 89004 CD: Claremont GSE 78-50-26 CD: Music and Arts CD 5026 CD: Legato LCD 146

Soll ich lauschen?

| London
May 1929 | Melchior
LSO
Coates | 78: HMV D 1724
78: Electrola EJ 483
78: Victor 7274
LP: HMV COLH 132/HLM 7026
LP: Electrola WCLP 799/E 83386
LP: Preiser LV 30
LP: EMI 1C 147 01259-01260M
LP: EMI RLS 7711/EX 29 02123
LP: Danacord DACO 119-120
CD: Danacord DACOCD 315-316
CD: EMI CMS 764 0082
CD: Preiser 89004
CD: Claremont GSE 78-50-26
CD: Music and Arts CD 5026
CD: Legato LCD 146 |

Die Walküre, unspecified extracts

Bayreuth August 1934	Role of Brünnhilde Müller, Bockelmann Bayreuth Festival Orchestra Elmendorff	LP: Ed Smith UORC 264

2 unpublished Met broadcasts may survive: according to Metropolitan Opera Annals live relays with Leider in the role of Brünnhilde took place on 2 February 1932 and 3 February 1933

Die Walküre, Excerpt (Du bist der Lenz....to end Act 1, omitting only Sieglinde's final outcry Bist du Siegmund...die eigne Schwester gewannst du zueins mit dem Schwert!)

Berlin November 1923	Role of Sieglinde Melchior Orchestra Unnamed conductor	78: Polydor 72868 & 72934/ 76565-76566 LP: DG 2548 749 LP: Danacord DACO 117-118 CD: Danacord DACOCD 313-314 CD: Preiser 89301 Du bist der Lenz only LP: DG 2700 708

Die Walküre: Excerpt (Nun zäume dein Ross-Hojotoho! Hojotoho!)

Berlin September 1927	Schorr Staatskapelle Blech	78: HMV D 1323 78: Electrola EJ 205 78: Victor 9167 LP: HMV COLH 105 LP: Electrola WCLP 799/E 83386 LP: Electrola E 83387-83388 LP: Toshiba GR 2124-2125 LP: Preiser LV 1370 LP: EMI 1C 147 30785-30786M LP: EMI RLS 7711 CD: Pearl GEMMCD 9357 CD: Claremont GSE 78-50-35/36

Die Walküre: Excerpt (Hojotoho! Hojotoho!)

London June 1938	Thorborg, Kamann LPO Furtwängler	LP: Ed Smith EJS 170/UORC 234

Die Walküre: Excerpt (O heilige Schmach!)

Berlin September 1927	Schorr Staatskapelle Blech	78: HMV D 1324 78: Electrola EJ 206 78: Victor 9168 CD: Pearl GEMMCD 9357 CD: Claremont GSE 78-50-35/36

Die Walküre: Excerpt (So nimm' meinen Segen, Niblungensohn)

Berlin September 1927	Schorr Staatskapelle Blech	78: HMV D 1324 78: Electrola EJ 206 78: Victor 9168 LP: Preiser LV 125 CD: Pearl GEMMCD 9357 CD: Claremont GSE 78-50-35/36

Die Walküre: Excerpt (Siegmund, sieh' auf mich!)

Berlin 1925	Soot Orchestra Unnamed conductor	78: Polydor 72986 LP: Preiser LV 155 CD: Preiser 89301

Die Walküre: Excerpt (Rette mich, Kühne!)

Berlin November 1927	Ljungberg Staatskapelle Blech	78: HMV DB 1329 78: Electrola EJ 209 78: Victor 9173 LP: EMI 1C 147 30785-30786M LP: Preiser LV 1370 CD: Pearl GEMMCD 9357 CD: Claremont GSE 78-50-35/36

Die Walküre: Excerpt (Wo ist Brünnhild'? Wo die Verbrecherin?)

Berlin October 1927	Schorr Staatskapelle Blech	78: HMV D 1330 78: Electrola EJ 212 78: Victor 9174 LP: Preiser LV 125 CD: Pearl GEMMCD 9357 CD: Claremont GSE 78-50-35/36

Die Walküre: Excerpt (Du verstössest mich?)

Berlin October 1927	Schorr Staatskapelle Blech	78: HMV D 1330 78: Electrola EJ 212 78: Victor 9174 LP: Preiser LV 125 CD: Pearl GEMMCD 9357 CD: Claremont GSE 78-50-35/36

Die Walküre: Excerpt (War es so schmählich, was ich verbrach?)

Berlin 1925	Orchestra Unnamed conductor	78: Polydor 72978 LP: Scala (USA) 835 LP: Rococo 5228 LP: Preiser LV 155 LP: Eterna 820 795 CD: Preiser 89301
Berlin November 1927	Staatskapelle Blech	78: HMV D 1331 78: Electrola EJ 213 78: Victor 9175 LP: HMV COLH 105 LP: Electrola E 80665 LP: EMI 1C 147 30785-30786M LP: EMI 1C 037 32201 LP: EMI RLS 7711 LP: Preiser LV 1370 CD: Pearl GEMMCD 9357 CD: Claremont GSE 78-50-35/36

Die Walküre: Excerpt (Du zeugtest ein edles Geschlecht)

Berlin November 1927	Schorr Staatskapelle Blech	78: HMV D 1331 78: Electrola EJ 213 78: Victor 9175 LP: HMV COLH 105 LP: EMI 1C 147 30785-30786M LP: EMI 1C 181 30669-30678M CD: Pearl GEMMCD 9357 CD: Claremont GSE 78-5--35/36

Der Engel (Wesendonk-Lieder)

Berlin	Orchestra	78: Polydor 72979
1926	Unnamed conductor	LP: Preiser LV 172
		LP: Rococo 5228
		LP: Eterna 820 795
		CD: Preiser 89301

Im Treibhaus (Wesendonk-Lieder)

Berlin	Orchestra	78: Polydor 72979
1926	Unnamed conductor	LP: Preiser LV 172
		LP: Rococo 5228
		LP: Eterna 820 795
		CD: Preiser 89301

Schmerzen (Wesendonk-Lieder)

Berlin	Orchestra	78: Polydor 65746
1922	Unnamed conductor	LP: Preiser LV 172
		CD: Preiser 89301
London	LSO	78: HMV DB 1553
May 1931	Barbirolli	78: Victor 7707
		LP: Preiser LV 1370
		LP: EMI 1C 147 30785-30786M
		LP: EMI EX 29 01693
		CD: Preiser 89004

Träume (Wesendonk-Lieder)

Berlin	Orchestra	78: Polydor 65746
1922	Unnamed conductor	LP: Preiser LV 172
		CD: Preiser 89301
London	Orchestra	78: HMV DB 1553
May 1928	Barbirolli	78: Victor 7707
		LP: Electrola WCLP 799/E 83386
		LP: EMI 1C 147 30785-30786M
		LP: Preiser LV 1370
		CD: Preiser 89004

Weber

Oberon: Excerpt (Ozean, du Ungeheuer!)

Berlin 1921	Orchestra Unnamed conductor	78: Polydor 65625 LP: Scala (USA) 835 LP: Preiser LV 240 LP: EMI RLS 743 CD: Preiser 89301

Wolf

Kennst du das Land? (Mignon)

Berlin January 1942	Raucheisen, piano	LP: EMI 1C 147 30785-30786M LP: Preiser LV 1370 This recording was not approved by the artist

Wie glänzt der helle Mond

Berlin January 1942	Raucheisen, piano	LP: Preiser LV 145 LP: EMI 1C 147 30785-30786M Also issued by the singer herself on a private acetate with a spoken greeting to her English friends

Miscellaneous

Frida Leider: Die goldene Stimme

Leider talks in German about her career and music	LP: Electrola WCLP 799/E 83386 With musical illustrations (see under Beethoven, Mozart, Schubert, Schumann and Wagner)

Kirsten Flagstad
1895-1962

with valuable assistance from
Clifford Elkin and Malcolm Walker

Discography compiled by John Hunt

Introduction

The discography of Kirsten Flagstad says it all: a far-reaching generosity, both in the huge repertory covered and also in the ample and re-assuring evenness of tone produced over a recording career of almost 40 years. This stretched from those first song recordings of the 1920s, produced for the local market, to those tonally resplendent Decca products of Flagstad's Indian summer.

With Decca at the end, as with HMV/Victor in the 20 years of her peak career, Kirsten Flagstad obviously gave the most scrupulous thought to what was set down on record. Is this an aspect of the same seriousness of purpose and dedication which led some critics of her stage performances to detect a coldness and calculation, even a lack of emotional involvement ? What this listener hears is a regal dignity above all, which may well not have been easily compatible with the heady and reckless comportment of some of her soprano colleagues at the Metropolitan in the late 1930s !

Flagstad herself always maintained that she was merely reproducing what the composer had set down, and for recordings she combined this with a circumspect awareness of the gramophone's potential. The special cause which she knowingly pleaded, outside her central work as the great Wagnerian of her age (along with Lauritz Melchior), was the cause of Scandinavian song, primarily but not exclusively from her native Norway.

There are the first local recordings in Norway, then a series for HMV/Victor where she insists on recording Grieg songs not only in the (for those times) standard German Translation but also in their native language (these recordings continued into the early post-war period, either with her long-standing friend and colleague Edwin McArthur or with Gerald Moore at the piano). Then, at Decca's behest following her rupture with HMV after indiscretions which she considered violated the confidence between artist and recording company, a veritable harvest of Scandinavian song both with piano and orchestral accompaniment. Nor was the German Lied neglected in all this, although some critics again found her to be a little too artless in her interpretations - there is no accounting for taste !

My special thanks while working on this discography goes to Terje Thorp for checking the countless Norwegian song titles - any spelling mistakes that remain are, of course, mine.

John Hunt

ROYAL ALBERT HALL

Manager: C. S. Taylor

PHILHARMONIA
ORCHESTRA

Founder and Artistic Director: WALTER LEGGE
Leader: MAX SALPETER

DR. WILHELM
FURTWÄNGLER

KIRSTEN
FLAGSTAD

SCHUMANN:	Manfred Overture
SCHUMANN:	Symphony No. 4
RAVEL:	Rhapsodie Espagnol

INTERVAL

WAGNER:	Five Wesendonck Songs
WAGNER:	Closing Scene from Götterdämmerung

Thursday, April 24, 1952

Management: IBBS & TILLETT LTD., 124 WIGMORE STREET, W.1

Aarmes

Haer vil eg kvile

Oslo
November 1954

Alme, piano

LP: Ed Smith UORC 243

Alnaes

De hundrede violiner

London January 1959	LSO Fjeldstad	LP: Decca LXT 5558/SXL 2145 LP: Decca BR 3059 LP: Decca ADD 209/SDD 209

Februarmorgen ved golfen

Oslo November 1954	Alme, piano	LP: Ed Smith UORC 243
London January 1959	LSO Fjeldstad	LP: Decca LXT 5558/SXL 2145 LP: Decca ADD 209/SDD 209

Lykken mellem to mennesker

Oslo January 1929	Alnaes, piano	78: HMV (Scandinavia) X 2974 LP: Harvest H 1004 LP: Legendary LR 120 CD: Legendary LRCD 1015 CD: EMI CDH 763 3052
Copenhagen July 1936	McArthur, piano	78: HMV DA 1516 78: Victor M 342 LP: Danacord DACO 168 CD: Danacord DACOCD 325 CD: Pearl GEMMCD 9092

Nu brister i alle kloefter

London January 1959	LSO Fjeldstad	LP: Decca LXT 5558/SXL 2145 LP: Decca ADD 209/SDD 209

Vaarlengsler

London January 1959	LSO Fjeldstad	LP: Decca LXT 5558/SXL 2145 LP: Decca ADD 209/SDD 209

C.P.E. Bach

<u>An dir allein, arr. Doerumsgaard</u>

London   Moore, piano   HMV unpublished
December 1952

<u>Preis sei dem Gotte, arr. Doerumsgaard</u>

London   Moore, piano   LP: Victor LHMV 1070
December 1952   LP: Pathé FALP 540

<u>Wie, Schönster, arr. Doerumsgaard</u>

London   Moore, piano   LP: Victor LHMV 1070
December 1952   LP: Pathé FALP 540

Bach

Saint Matthew Passion: Excerpt (Erbarme dich, mein Gott)

London
June 1950

Philharmonia
Süsskind

78: HMV DB 21237
45: HMV 7R 126
LP: HMV HQM 1057
LP: EMI 1C 147 01491-01492M
LP: Toshiba GR 2172
LP: EMI EX 29 02051
CD: Testament SBT 1018

Saint Matthew Passion: Excerpt (Blute nur, du liebes Herz)

London
December 1956

LPO
Boult
Sung in English

LP: Decca LXT 5316

Bist du bei mir

London
December 1956

LPO
Boult
Sung in English

LP: Decca LXT 5316

Jesu bleibet meine Freude (Cantata No 147)

London
December 1956

LPO
Boult
Sung in English

45: Decca CEP 540
LP: Decca LXT 5316

Komm, süsser Tod, arr. Doerumsgaard

London
June 1950

Moore, piano

78: HMV DB 21490
LP: Victor LHMV 1070
LP: Pathé FALP 540

Schafe können sicher weiden (Cantata No 208)

London
December 1956

LPO
Boult
Sung in English

45: Decca CEP 540
LP: Decca LXT 5316

Liebster Herr Jesu, arr. Doerumsgaard

London
December 1952

Moore, piano

LP: Victor LHMV 1070
LP: Pathé FALP 540

O finstre Nacht, arr. Doerumsgaard

London
December 1952

Moore, piano

LP: Victor LHMV 1070
LP: Pathé FALP 540

Backer-Groendahl

Det aer vackrast naer det skymmer

Oslo November 1954	Alme, piano	LP: Ed Smith UORC 243

Endnu et streif kun av sol

Oslo 1926	Orchestra Unnamed conductor	78: Odeon (Scandinavia) LP: Harvest H 1004 LP: Legendary LR 120 CD: Legendary LRCD 1015 <u>Harvest dates this as 1924</u>

Mot kveld

Oslo October 1923	Orchestra Unnamed conductor	78: HMV (Scandinavia) X 1946 LP: Harvest H 1004 LP: Legendary LR 120 CD: Legendary LRCD 1015 CD: EMI CDH 763 3052 CD: Memories HR 4456-4457
New York April 1936	McArthur, piano	78: HMV DA 1520 LP: Danacord DACO 168 CD: Danacord DACOCD 325 CD: Pearl GEMMCD 9092

Og det traedje fottrin

Oslo November 1954	Alme, piano	LP: Ed Smith UORC 243

Beethoven

New York December 1938	Role of Leonore Farell, Laufkötter, Maison, Schorr, List, Gabor Metropolitan Orchestra & Chorus Bodansky	LP: Melodram MEL 307 CD: Music and Arts CD 619 This performance contains Bodansky's own composed recitatives in place of the spoken dialogue
New York February 1941	Role of Leonore Farell, Laufkötter, Maison, Janssen, Kipnis, Huehn Metropolitan Orchestra & Chorus Walter	Unpublished radio broadcast Abscheulicher CD: Memories HR 4456-4457
Salzburg August 1949	Role of Leonore Seefried, Holm, Patzak, Greindl, Schöffler, Braun VPO Vienna Opera Chorus Furtwängler	Unpublished radio broadcast
Salzburg August 1950	Role of Leonore Schwarzkopf, Dermota, Patzak, Greindl, Schöffler, Braun VPO Vienna Opera Chorus Furtwängler	LP: Morgan MOR 5001 LP: MRF 50/BJR 112 LP: Discocorp IGI 328 LP: Cetra FE 44 CD: Hunt CDWFE 304/CDWFE 354 CD: Verona 27044-27045 CD: EMI CHS 764 9012
New York March 1951	Role of Leonore Connor, Klein, Svanholm, Ernster, Schöffler, Hines Metropolitan Orchestra & Chorus Walter	LP: Discocorp RR 804

Fidelio: Excerpt (Abscheulicher, wo eilst du hin?)

Philadelphia October 1937	Philadelphia Orchestra Ormandy	78: Victor 14972 78: HMV DB 3439 LP: RCA CAL 462 LP: Preiser LV 1372 CD: Nimbus NI 7847/Memoir CDMOIR 408 CD: Pickwick GLRS 105
London May 1951	Covent Garden Orchestra Rankl	LP: Ed Smith EJS 390

Fidelio: Excerpt (Mir ist so wunderbar)

London May 1951	Schwarzkopf, Stevenson, Gwynne Covent Garden Orchestra/Rankl	LP: Ed Smith EJS 390 Quartet is preceded and followed by dialogue spoken in English

Ah perfido !

Philadelphia October 1937	Philadelphia Orchestra Ormandy	78: Victor M 439 78: HMV DB 3441 and DA 1625 LP: RCA CAL 462 LP: RCA VIC 1208/VIC 1517 LP: RCA PVM1-9068/AG 26.41399 LP: Preiser LV 1372 CD: Nimbus NI 7847/Pickwick GLRS 105 78 issues comprised 1 12" and 1 10" record
Havana 1948	Havana PO Krauss	CD: Eklipse EKRCD 15

Gellert-Lieder

Oslo September 1954	Alme, piano	LP: Harvest H 1005

Die Ehre Gottes aus der Natur (Gellert-Lieder)

Copenhagen July 1936	McArthur, piano	78: Victor M 342 78: HMV DB 1514 CD: Pearl GEMMCD 9092

Andenken

Oslo September 1954	Alme, piano	LP: Anna ANNA 1025

An die Hoffnung

Oslo September 1954	Alme, piano	CD: Acanta 43.189 Also published by Acanta on LP

Ich liebe dich

Copenhagen July 1936	McArthur, piano	78: Victor M 342 78: HMV DB 1514 CD: Pearl GEMMCD 9092
New York January 1953	McArthur, piano	LP: Victor LM 1738 LP: HMV ALP 1191
Oslo September 1954	Alme, piano	LP: Anna ANNA 1025

Wonne der Wehmut

Oslo September 1954	Alme, piano	LP: Anna ANNA 1025

Bishop

Home, sweet home

Oslo
1926

Pianist unnamed
Sung in Norwegian

78: Odeon (Scandinavia) 5371
LP: Harvest H 1004
LP: Legendary LR 120
CD: Legendary LRCD 1015
Harvest dates this as 1924

Bizet

Agnus Dei

London
July 1948

Philharmonia
W. Braithwaite

78: HMV DB 6791

Bohm

Geh' ein, mein' Lieb', in deine Kammer

London
December 1952

Moore, piano

LP: Victor LHMV 1070
LP: Pathé FALP 540

Still wie die Nacht

New York
October 1937

Iturbi, piano

LP: Legendary LR 120
CD: Legendary LRCD 1015

Brahms

Alte Liebe

London
August 1956

McArthur, piano

LP: Decca LXT 5345

Am Sonntag Morgen

London
August 1956

McArthur, piano

LP: Decca LXT 5345

Auf dem Kirchhofe

London
August 1956

McArthur, piano

LP: Decca LXT 5345

Bei dir sind meine Gedanken

London
August 1956

McArthur, piano

LP: Decca LXT 5345

Dein blaues Auge

London
August 1956

McArthur, piano

LP: Decca LXT 5345

Geistliches Wiegenlied

London
June 1949

Moore, piano
Downes, viola

78: HMV DA 1933
45: HMV 7EB 6012
LP: Seraphim 60046
LP: EMI RLS 154 7003

Gestillte Sehnsucht

London June 1949	Moore, piano Downes, viola	78: HMV DA 1932 45: HMV 7EB 6012 LP: Seraphim 60046

Liebestreu

New York March 1953	McArthur, piano	LP: Victor LM 1870 LP: HMV ALP 1309

Meine Liebe ist grün

London June 1937	McArthur, piano	78: HMV DA 1586 LP: EMI RLS 154 7003 CD: Pearl GEMMCD 9092
New York March 1953	McArthur, piano	LP: Victor LM 1870 LP: HMV ALP 1309

Muss es eine Trennung geben?

New York   McArthur, piano   LP: Victor LM 2825
April 1952

O wüsst' ich doch den Weg zurück

New York   McArthur, piano   LP: Victor LM 1738
January 1953   LP: HMV ALP 1191

Sind es Schmerzen (Magelone-Lieder)

New York   McArthur, piano   LP: Victor LM 1870
March 1953   LP: HMV ALP 1309

Treue Liebe

London   McArthur, piano   LP: Decca LXT 5345
August 1956

4 ernste Gesänge

London   McArthur, piano   LP: Decca LXT 5345
November 1956

Von ewiger Liebe

New York   McArthur, piano   LP: Victor LM 1738
January 1953   LP: HMV ALP 1191

Wie froh und frisch

New York   McArthur, piano   LP: Victor LM 2825
April 1952

Wie Melodien zieht es mir

London   McArthur, piano   LP: Decca LXT 5345
August 1956

Wir wandelten

London   McArthur, piano   LP: Decca LXT 5345
August 1956

Bridge

Love went a' riding

London June 1937	McArthur, piano	78: HMV DA 1588 LP: EMI EX 29 09113
New York October 1937	Iturbi, piano	LP: Legendary LR 120 CD: Legendary LRCD 1015

Bull

Saeterjentens soendag

Oslo October 1923	Orchestra	78: HMV (Scandinavia) X 1940 LP: Harvest H 1004 LR: Legendary LR 120 CD: Legendary LRCD 1015
Oslo January 1929	Orchestra	78: HMV (Scandinavia) X 2975 LP: Harvest H 1004 CD: EMI CDH 763 3052

Carissimi

Soccorretemi ch' io moro, arr. Doerumsgaard

London June 1950	Moore, piano	78: HMV DA 2008 LP: Pathé FALP 540

Carpenter

When I bring you coloured toys

New York   McArthur, piano   LP: Victor LM 2825
March 1952

The sleep that flits on baby's eyes

New York   McArthur, piano   LP: Victor LM 2825
March 1952

Charles

When I have sung my songs

Copenhagen   McArthur, piano   78: HMV DA 1524
October 1936   78: Victor M 342
                                            LP: New World NW 247
                                            CD: Pearl GEMMCD 9092

New York   McArthur, piano   LP: Victor LM 1738
January 1953   LP: HMV ALP 1191

Crüger

Nu la oss takke Gud

Oslo   Fotland, organ   LP: Decca LXT 5662
September 1956   LP: Simax (Norway) PS 1801

Deems Taylor

A song for lovers (Songs from the Clay)

New York   McArthur, piano   LP: Victor LM 1870
March 1953   LP: HMV ALP 1309

Doerumsgaard

Baan sull

London
December 1952
Moore, piano
LP: HMV ALP 1140

Blaakveld

London
December 1952
Moore, piano
LP: HMV ALP 1140

Det er fjord i millom frendar

London
December 1952
Moore, piano
LP: HMV ALP 1140

Oslo
November 1954
Alme, piano
LP: Ed Smith UORC 243

En hustavle

London
December 1952
Moore, piano
LP: HMV ALP 1140

Et barn

London
December 1952
Moore, piano
LP: HMV ALP 1140

Fattig er mitt liv

Oslo
November 1954
Alme, piano
LP: Ed Smith UORC 243

Gudrid stod ved stoveglas

London
December 1952
Moore, piano
LP: HMV ALP 1140

Hjuring-lokk

London
December 1952
Moore, piano
LP: HMV ALP 1140

Konn og guld

London
December 1952
Moore, piano
LP: HMV ALP 1140

Kvelding

London
December 1952

Moore, piano

LP: HMV ALP 1140

Kviteis i sudroena

London
December 1952

Moore, piano

LP: HMV ALP 1140

Natt

London
December 1952

Moore, piano

LP: HMV ALP 1140

2 norske folkeviser

London
December 1952

Moore, piano

LP: HMV ALP 1140

Regn

London
December 1952

Moore, piano

LP: HMV ALP 1140

Salme

London
December 1952

Moore, piano

LP: HMV ALP 1140

4 sanger under stjernen

London
December 1952

Moore, piano

LP: HMV ALP 1140

Soevnen

London
December 1952

Moore, piano

LP: HMV ALP 1140

Snoelyse

London
December 1952

Moore, piano

LP: HMV ALP 1140

Spinnvettir

London
December 1952

Moore, piano

LP: HMV ALP 1140

Duncan

Jubilate, arr. Woodgate

London   LPO   45: Decca SEC 5002
April 1957   Boult   LP: Decca LXT 5392/SXL 2049
                                            LP: Decca ADD 207/SDD 207

Dvorak

Songs my mother taught me

Copenhagen   McArthur, piano   78: HMV DA 1524
July 1936   Sung in English   78: Victor DA 2009
                                            CD: Pearl GEMMCD 9092

Dykes

Holy, holy, holy

Oslo   Fotland, organ   LP: Decca LXT 5662
September 1956   LP: Simax (Norway) PS 1801

Eggen

Aerer det evige foraar i livet

London   LSO   LP: Decca LXT 5558/SXL 2145
January 1959   Fjeldstad   LP: Decca ADD 209/SDD 209

Foster

<u>Old folks at home</u>

New York	Orchestra	LP: Legendary LR 120 /LR 142
October 1937	Chorus	CD: Legendary LRCD 1015
	Iturbi	

J.W. Franck

<u>Sei nur still...auf zu Gottes Lob, arr. Doerumsgaard</u>

London	Moore, piano	78: HMV DA 2008
June 1950		LP: Victor LHMV 1070
		LP: Pathé FALP 540

<u>Wie sah ich dich, arr. Doerumsgaard</u>

London	Moore, piano	HMV unpublished
December 1952		

Franz

<u>Im Herbst</u>

London	McArthur, piano	78: HMV DB 3305
June 1937		78: Victor 15645

Freylinghausen

<u>Es ist vollbracht, arr. Doerumsgaard</u>

London	Moore, piano	LP: Victor LHMV 1070
December 1952		LP: Pathé FALP 540

WAGNER

Götterdämmerung

Brünnhilde	KIRSTEN FLAGSTAD
Siegfried	SET SVANHOLM
Hagen	EGIL NORDSJØ
Gunther	WALDEMAR JOHNSEN
Waltraute	EVA GUSTAVSON

THE OSLO PHILHARMONIC ORCHESTRA
THE NORWEGIAN STATE RADIO ORCHESTRA
THE OPERA CHORUS
conducted by OIVIN FJELDSTAD

LXT 5205-10

A German-English libretto is available with a thematic index, price 7/6 from dealers or direct from us.

Special Advance Announcement

DIE WALKÜRE

A really sensational performance and recording of Act III is to be released shortly. The soloists are KIRSTEN FLAGSTAD, OTTO EDELMANN, MARIANNE SCHECH, ODA BALSBORG, ILONA STEINGRUBER, GRACE HOFFMANN, MARGARET BENCE, CLARE WATSON, ANNY DELORIE, FREEDA ROESLER, HETTY PLUMACHER with *THE VIENNA PHILHARMONIC ORCHESTRA* conducted by GEORG SOLTI.

DECCA RECORDS

THE DECCA RECORD COMPANY LTD
1-3 BRIXTON ROAD LONDON S W 9

Gjerstroem

Nocturne

Oslo November 1954	Alme, piano	LP: Ed Smith UORC 243

Gluck

Alceste

London April and May 1956	Role of Alceste Lowe, Jobin, Young, Hemsley Geraint Jones Orchestra & Singers G.Jones Sung in Italian	LP: Decca LXT 5273-5276 LP: Decca GOM 574-576/GOS 574-576 CD: Decca 436 2342
Copenhagen April 1957	Role of Alceste Engeboll, Arstrop, Christianson, Mollner Danish Radio Orchestra & Chorus Hye-Knudsen Sung in Norwegian	CD: Eklipse EKRCD 24 Excerpts CD: Melodram MEL 26514

An unpublished Met broadcast may still be preserved: according to Metropolitan Opera Annals a live relay with Flagstad in the role of Alceste took place on 29 March 1952 (one of her final Metropolitan appearances)

Alceste: Excerpt (Divinités du Styx)

Oslo 1960	Orchestra Sung in Norwegian	LP: Legendary LR 120 CD: Legendary LRCD 1015 Flagstad's last public appearance

Orfeo ed Euridice: Excerpt (Che farò)

London May 1948	Philharmonia Süsskind	78: HMV DB 6913 45: HMV 7R 164 LP: HMV HQM 1057 LP: EMI 1C 147 01491-01492M LP: EMI EX 29 02061 CD: Testament SBT 1018

Gounod

O divine redeemer

London April 1957	LPO Boult	45: Decca CEP 517 LP: Decca LXT 5392.SXL 2092 LP: Decca ADD 209/SDD 209

Grieg

Borte

Oslo June 1954	Alme, piano	LP: Ed Smith EJS 390

Den aergjerrige

London April 1956	McArthur, piano	LP: Decca LXT 5264/ECS 622

Den saerde

London April 1948	Philharmonia W.Braithwaite	78: HMV DB 21020 LP: HMV HQM 1057/Toshiba GR 2172 LP: EMI 1C 147 01491-01492M CD: EMI CDH 763 3052

Der gynger en baad paa boelge

Copenhagen July 1936	McArthur, piano	78: HMV DA 1515 LP: Danacord DACO 168 CD: Danacord DACOCD 325 CD: Pearl GEMMCD 9092
Oslo June 1954	Alme, piano	LP: Ed Smith EJS 390
London April 1956	McArthur, piano	LP: Decca LXT 5264/ECS 622

Det foerste moete

London April 1956	McArthur, piano	LP: Decca LXT 5264/ECS 622
London September 1957	BBC SO Sargent	LP: Ed Smith UORC 264 LP: Rococo 5380 CD: AS-Disc AS 360 CD: Memories HR 4456-4457

Efteraarstormen

London May 1948	Moore, piano	45: HMV 7EB 6007 LP: Seraphim 60046
Oslo June 1954	Alme, piano	LP: Ed Smith EJS 390
London January 1959	LSO Fjeldstad	LP: Decca LXT 5558/SXL 2145 LP: Decca ADD 209/SDD 209 CD: Decca 425 5122

En droem

New York April 1936	McArthur, piano	CD: RCA/BMG 09026 618792/ 09026 618272 Previously unpublished
Copenhagen July 1936	McArthur, piano Sung in German	78: HMV DA 1505 78: Victor 1804 LP: Danacord DACO 168 CD: Danacord DACOCD 325 CD: Pearl GEMMCD 9092
London April 1948	Philharmonia W.Braithwaite	78: HMV DB 21020 CD: EMI CDH 763 3052
Bergen June 1953	Oslo PO Gruner-Hegge	CD: Eklipse EKRCD 15
London April 1956	McArthur, piano	45: Decca CEP 563 LP: Decca LXT 5264/ECS 622

En svane

Copenhagen July 1936	McArthur, piano Sung in German	78: HMV DA 1513 LP: Danacord DACO 168 CD: Danacord DACOCD 325 CD: Pearl GEMMCD 9092
London March 1948	Philharmonia W.Braithwaite	78: HMV DA 1879 45: Victor WDM 1533 LP: Victor LM 99 LP: HMV HQM 1057/Toshiba GR 2172 LP: EMI 1C 147 01491-01492M CD: EMI CDH 763 3052
London September 1957	BBC SO Sargent	LP: Ed Smith UORC 264 CD: AS-Disc AS 360 CD: Memories HR 4456-4457

Eros

London March 1948	Philharmonia W.Braithwaite	78: HMV DA 1879 45: Victor WDM 1533 LP: Victor LM 99 CD: EMI CDH 763 3052
London April 1956	McArthur, piano	LP: Decca LXT 5264 LP: Decca BR 3059/ECS 622
London September 1957	BBC SO Sargent	LP: Ed Smith UORC 264 CD: AS-Disc AS 360 CD: Memories HR 4456-4457

Et haab

Copenhagen July 1936	McArthur, piano	78: HMV DA 1516 78: Victor M 342 LP: Danacord DACO 168 CD: Danacord DACOCD 325 CD: Pearl GEMMCD 9092
London October 1953	Moore, piano	HMV unpublished
Oslo June 1954	Alme, piano	LP: Ed Smith EJS 390
London September 1957	BBC SO Sargent	LP: Ed Smith UORC 264 LP: Rococo 5380 CD: AS-Disc AS 360 CD: Memories HR 4456-4457

Fra Monte Pincio

London March 1948	Philharmonia W.Braithwaite	HMV unpublished
London May 1948	Philharmonia W.Braithwaite	78: HMV DA 1905 45: HMV 7EB 6011 45: Victor WDM 1533 LP: Victor LM 99 CD: EMI CDH 763 3052 DA 1905 was probably not published
Bergen June 1953	Oslo PO Gruner-Hegge	CD: Eklipse EKRCD 15
London April 1956	McArthur, piano	45: Decca CEP 563 LP: Decca LXT 5264/ECS 622
London September 1957	BBC SO Sargent	LP: Ed Smith UORC 264 CD: AS-Disc AS 360 CD: Memories HR 4456-4457

Fyremaal

London May 1948	Moore, piano	45: HMV 7EB 6007 LP: Seraphim 60046
London September 1957	BBC SO Sargent	LP: Ed Smith UORC 264 LP: Rococo 5380 CD: AS-Disc AS 360 CD: Memories HR 4456-4457

Guten, orch. Gunstrom

London May 1948	Philharmonia W.Braithwaite	78: HMV DA 1992 45: Victor WDM 1533 LP: Victor LM 99 CD: EMI CDH 763 3052
London September 1957	BBC SO Sargent	LP: Ed Smith UORC 264 CD: AS-Disc AS 360 CD: Memories HR 4456-4457

Haugtussa, song cycle: 1.Det syng; 2.Veslemoey; 3.Blaaboerli; 4.Moete; 5.Elsk; 6.Killingdans; 7.Vond dag; 8.Ved gjoetle-bekken

New York 1940	McArthur, piano	78: HMV DB 5833-5836 78: Victor M 714 LP: Victor LM 1094
New York April 1950	McArthur, piano	LP: Victor LM 2825 CD: RCA/BMG 09026 618792 (3 and 8)/ 09026 618272 (3 and 8)
London November 1956	McArthur, piano	LP: Decca LXT 5327/ECS 623

Hytten

London March 1956	McArthur, piano	45: Decca CEP 563 LP: Decca LXT 5264/ECS 622

Jeg elsker dig

New York April 1936	McArthur, piano	CD: RCA/BMG 09026 618792/ 09026 618272 Previously unpublished
New York April 1936	McArthur, piano Sung in German	78: HMV DA 1505 78: Victor 1804 LP: Danacord DACO 168 CD: Danacord DACOCD 325 CD: Pearl GEMMCD 9092
Copenhagen July 1936	McArthur, piano	78: HMV DA 1520 LP: Danacord DACO 168 CD: Danacord DACOCD 325 CD: Pearl GEMMCD 9092
Oslo June 1954	Alme, piano	LP: Ed Smith EJS 390
London March 1956	McArthur, piano	45: Decca CEP 563 LP: Decca LXT 5264/ECS 622
London September 1957	BBC SO Sargent	LP: Ed Smith UORC 264 LP: Rococo 5380 CD: AS-Disc AS 360 CD: Memories HR 4456-4457

Jeg giver mit digt til vaaren

London October 1953	Moore, piano	HMV unpublished
London March 1956	McArthur, piano	LP: Decca LXT 5264/ECS 622
London November 1956	LSO Fjeldstad	LP: Decca LXT 5558/SXL 2145 LP: Decca BR 3059 LP: Decca ADD 209/SDD 209 CD: Decca 425 5122

Langs ei aa

London May 1948	Moore, piano	45: HMV 7EB 6007 LP: Seraphim 60046

Liden hoejt deroppe

Oslo June 1954	Alme, piano	LP: Ed Smith EJS 390
London March 1956	McArthur, piano	LP: Decca LXT 5264/ECS 622

Liden Kirsten

London March 1956	McArthur, piano	LP: Decca LXT 5264/ECS 622

Lys natt

Copenhagen July 1936	McArthur, piano	78: HMV DA 1515 78: Victor M 342 LP: HMV HQM 1057/Toshiba GR 2172 LP: Danacord DACO 168 CD: Danacord DACOCD 325 CD: Pearl GEMMCD 9092 Pearl incorrectly states that this song is performed with orchestra cond. Braithwaite
Bergen June 1953	Oslo PO Gruner-Hegge	CD: Eklipse EKRCD 15
Oslo June 1954	Alme, piano	LP: Ed Smith EJS 390

Med en primula veris

London June 1937	McArthur, piano	78: HMV DB 3392 CD: EMI CDH 763 3052 CD: Pearl GEMMCD 9092
London March 1956	McArthur, piano	45: Decca CEP 563 LP: Decca LXT 5264/ECS 622

Med en vandlilje

New York April 1936	McArthur, piano	CD: RCA/BMG 09026 618792/ 09026 618272 Previously unpublished
London May 1948	Moore, piano	78: HMV DA 1957 LP: HMV HQM 1057/Toshiba GR 2172 CD: EMI CDH 763 3052
London March 1956	McArthur, piano	LP: Decca LXT 5264/ECS 622

Mens jeg venter

Copenhagen July 1936	McArthur, piano <u>Sung in German</u>	78: HMV DA 1513 78: Victor M 342 CD: Pearl GEMMCD 9092
London May 1948	Moore, piano	45: HMV 7EB 6007 LP: Seraphim 60046

Millom rosor

Oslo January 1929	Orchestra	78: HMV (Scandinavia) X 3068 LP: Harvest H 1004 LP: Legendary LR 120 CD: Legendary LRCD 1015 CD: EMI CDH 763 3052
London March 1956	McArthur, piano	LP: Decca LXT 5264/ECS 622

Modersorg

Oslo January 1929	Orchestra	78: HMV (Scandinavia) X 3068 LP: Harvest H 1004 LP: Legendary LR 120 CD: Legendary LRCD 1015 CD: EMI CDH 763 3052

Og jeg vil ha mig en Hjertenskjaer

London May 1937	McArthur, piano	78: HMV DB 3392 CD: EMI CDH 763 3052 CD: Pearl GEMMCD 9092
Oslo June 1954	Alme, piano	LP: Ed Smith EJS 390
London November 1956	LSO Fjeldstad	LP: Decca LXT 5558/SXL 2145 LP: Decca ADD 209/SDD 209 CD: Decca 425 5122

Prinsessen

London May 1948	Moore, piano	78: HMV DA 1957 LP: HMV HQM 1057/Toshiba GR 2172 CD: EMI CDH 763 3052

Solveigs Sang (Peer Gynt)

Oslo October 1923	Orchestra	78: HMV (Scandinavia) X 1940 LP: Harvest H 1004 LP: Legendary LR 120 CD: Legendary LRCD 1015
Oslo January 1929	Orchestra	78: HMV (Scandinavia) X 2975 LP: Harvest H 1004 CD: EMI CDH 763 3052

Tak for dit raad, orch. Kleven

London April 1948	Philharmonia W.Braithwaite	78: HMV DB 21020 LP: HMV HQM 1057/Toshiba GR 2172 LP: EMI 1C 147 01491-01492M CD: EMI CDH 763 3052

Til en I; Til en II

London January 1959	LSO Fjeldstad	LP: Decca LXT 5558/SXL 2145 LP: Decca ADD 209/SDD 209 CD: Decca 425 5122

Vaaren

Oslo 1926	Unnamed pianist	78: Odeon (Norway) 5348 LP: Harvest H 1004 LP: Legendary LR· 120 CD: Legendary LRCD 1015
London May 1948	Philharmonia Süsskind	78: HMV DA 1904 45: HMV 7EB 6011 45: Victor WDM 1533 LP: Victor LM 99 CD: EMI CDH 763 3052
London September 1957	BBC SO Sargent	LP: Ed Smith UORC 264/ANNA 1016 CD: AS-Disc AS 360 CD: Memories HR 4456-4457

Ved Rundarne, orch. Kleven

London April 1948	Philharmonia W.Braithwaite	78: HMV DA 1992 45: Victor WDM 1533 LP: Victor LM 99 CD: EMI CDH 763 3052
London September 1957	BBC SO Sargent	LP: Ed Smith UORC 264 CD: AS-Disc AS 360 CD: Memories HR 4456-4457

Gruber

Silent night

New York December 1937	Orchestra	LP: Legendary LR 120 CD: Legendary LRCD 1015 With Flagstad's introductory spoken comments
London April 1957	LPO Boult	45: Decca CEP 517/SEC 5002 LP: Decca LXT 5392/SXL 2049 LP: Decca ADD 207/SDD 207

Handel

Dank sei dir Herr, attrib.

London July 1948	Philharmonia W.Braithwaite	CD: Testament SBT 1018
London December 1956	LPO Boult Sung in English	LP: Decca LXT 5316 CD: Decca 436 2342

Messiah: Excerpt (He shall feed his flock)

London December 1956	LPO Boult	LP: Decca LXT 5316 CD: Decca 436 2342

Messiah: Excerpt (I know that my redeemer liveth)

London December 1956	LPO Boult	LP: Decca LXT 5316 CD: Decca 436 2342

Radamisto: Excerpt (Gods all powerful)

London December 1956	LPO Boult	LP: Decca LXT 5316 CD: Decca 436 2342

Semele: Excerpt (O sleep, why dost thou leave me?)

London December 1956	LPO Boult	LP: Decca LXT 5316 CD: Decca 436 2342

Serse: Excerpt (Ombra mai fù)

London July 1948	Philharmonia W.Braithwaite	78: HMV DB 6791 LP: EMI 1C 147 01491-01492M LP: EMI EX 29 02061

Head

The little road to Bethlehem

Oslo Alme, piano CD: Voce 120
September 1954

Hurum

Blonde netter

London McArthur, piano 78: HMV DB 3392
June 1937   CD: EMI CDH 763 3052
    CD: Pearl GEMMCD 9092
    CD: Memories HR 4456-4457

Hymne til solen

Oslo Alme, piano LP: Ed Smith UORC 243
November 1954

Jordan

Runde

Oslo Alme, piano LP: Ed Smith UORC 243
November 1954

Kielland

Den fyrste songen

Oslo Alme, piano LP: Ed Smith UORC 243
November 1954

Kjerulf

Aa reven laa under birkerot

Oslo 1926	Unnamed pianist	78: Odeon (Scandinavia) 5409

Da barnet sov inn

Oslo 1926	Unnamed pianist	78: Odeon (Scandinavia) 5552

Nu tak for alt (Synnoves Sang)

Oslo 1926	Unnamed pianist	78: Odeon (Scandinavia) 5409

Kramer

Now like a lantern

New York March 1952	McArthur, piano	LP: Victor LM 2825

Kvendal

Cantata

Oslo 1950	Orchestra	LP: Harvest H 1005

Liddle

Abide with me

London April 1957	LPO Boult	LP: Decca LXT 5392/SXL 2049 LP: Decca ADD 207/SDD 207

Lie

Sne

Oslo January 1929	Alnaes, piano	78: HMV (Scandinavia) X 2974 LP: Harvest H 1004 LP: Legendary LR 120 CD: Legendary LRCD 1015 CD: EMI CDH 763 3052 CD: Memories HR 4456-4457 Legendary issues incorrectly give composer's name as Rode

Nykelen

London January 1959	LSO Fjeldstad	LP: Decca LXT 5558/SXL 2145 LP: Decca ADD 209/SDD 209

Skinnveng-brev

London January 1959	LSO Fjeldstad	LP: Decca LXT 5558/SXL 2145 LP: Decca ADD 209/SDD 209

Lindeman

5 Norwegian Hymns: I prektige himler og jorderiks haere, arr. Alnaes;
Gud skal all ting lage, arr. Alnaes; Dype stille sterke milde, arr. Alnaes;
Paskemorgen slukker sorgen: Sorg o kjaere fader du

Oslo September 1956	Fotland, organ	LP: Decca LXT 5662 LP: Simax (Norway) PS 1801

Lohner

O Ewigkeit, arr. Dorumsgaard

London June 1950	Moore, piano	78: HMV DB 21490 LP: Pathé FALP 540
London December 1952	Moore, piano	HMV unpublished

Luther

Vaar Gud han er saa fast en borg, arr. Alnaes

Oslo September 1956	Fotland, organ	LP: Decca LXT 5662 LP: Simax (Norway) PS 1801

Mahler

Kindertotenlieder

Vienna May 1957	VPO Boult	LP: Decca LXT 5395/SXL 2224 LP: Decca BR 3031/ECS 780 CD: Decca 414 6242/440 4912

Lieder eines fahrenden Gesellen

Vienna May 1957	VPO Boult	45: Decca CEP 680/SEC 5079 LP: Decca LXT 5395/SXL 2224 LP: Decca ECS 780 CD: Decca 414 6242/440 4912

McArthur

Night

New York　　　　　　McArthur, piano　　　　LP: Victor LM 1870
March 1953　　　　　　　　　　　　　　　　　LP: HMV ALP 1309

We have turned again home

New York　　　　　　McArthur, piano　　　　LP: Victor LM 1738
January 1953　　　　　　　　　　　　　　　　LP: HMV ALP 1191

Mendelssohn

Hear my prayer

London　　　　　　　LPO　　　　　　　　　　LP: Decca LXT 5392/SXL 2049
April 1957　　　　　Boult　　　　　　　　　LP: Decca ADD 207/SDD 207

Saint Paul: Excerpt (Jerusalem)

London　　　　　　　LPO　　　　　　　　　　LP: Decca LXT 5392/SXL 2049
April 1957　　　　　Boult　　　　　　　　　LP: Decca ADD 207/SDD 207

Minsaas

Praeludium

Oslo　　　　　　　　Alme, piano　　　　　　LP: Ed Smith UORC 243
November 1954

Neander

Lover den Herre, arr. Lamb

Oslo
September 1956
Fotland, organ
LP: Decca LXT 5662
LP: Simax (Norway) PS 1801

Parry

Jerusalem

London
April 1957
LPO
Boult
45: Decca SEC 5002
LP: Decca LXT 5392/SXL 2049
LP: Decca ADD 207/SDD 207

Peaters

Da lyset slukket

Oslo
1926
Unnamed pianist
78: Odeon (Scandinavia) 5346

Purcell

Dido and Aeneas

London October, November and December 1951	Role of Dido Teyte, Mandikian, Lloyd, Hemsley Mermaid Orchestra and Singers G.Jones	5 complete performances recorded live HMV unpublished
London March 1952	Role of Dido Schwarzkopf, Mandikian, Lloyd, Hemsley Philharmonia Mermaid Singers G.Jones	45: Victor WHMV 1007 LP: Victor LHMV 1007 LP: HMV ALP 1026 LP: Electrola E 90031 LP: Seraphim 60346 LP: World Records SH 117 LP: EMI 2C 051 03613 CD: EMI CDH 761 0062 Orchestra described on all issues as Mermaid Orchestra; EMI CD issue gives recording date as October 1952

Dido and Aeneas, unspecified excerpts

Oslo March 1953	Buntz, Frisell Orchestra & Chorus Fjeldstad Sung in Norwegian	LP: Anna ANNA 1025

Dido and Aeneas, opening scene

London October 1952	Mermaid Orchestra and Singers G.Jones	LP: Ed Smith EJS 183

Dido and Aeneas: Excerpt (Thy hand Belinda....When I am laid in earth)

London May 1948	Philharmonia W.Braithwaite	78: HMV DB 6913 45: HMV 7R 164 LP: HMV HQM 1057 LP: EMI 1C 147 01491-01492M LP: Toshiba GR 2172 CD: Testament SBT 1018
London October 1952	Mermaid Orchestra and Singers G.Jones	LP: Ed Smith EJS 183 LP: Rococo 5380 LP: Legendary LR 120 CD: Legendary LRCD 1015 <u>This performance, which all issues incorrectly date as 1953, is followed by Flagstad's farewell speech from the stage</u>
Oslo March 1953	Orchestra Fjeldstad <u>Sung in Norwegian</u>	LP: Anna ANNA 1025 CD: Eklipse EKRCD 15 Eklipse dated 1955

Purday

Leid, milde ljos

Oslo September 1956	Fotland, organ	LP: Decca LXT 5662 LP: Simax (Norway) PS 1801

Rogers

At parting

London June 1937	McArthur, piano	78: HMV DA 1588 78: Victor 1890
New York January 1953	McArthur, piano	LP: Victor LM 1738 LP: HMV ALP 1191

Ronald

O lovely night

Oslo July 1936	McArthur, piano	78: HMV DA 1512 78: Victor 1890 CD: Pearl GEMMCD 9092
London February 1938	Orchestra & Chorus MacMillan	LP: Legendary LR 120 CD: Legendary LRCD 1015

Royal Opera Covent Garden

LONDON & PROVINCIAL OPERA SOCIETY SEASON
Artistic Director: Sir Thomas Beecham, Bart.
Secretary & Manager: Charles A. Barrand

Der Ring des Nibelungen
RICHARD WAGNER

Friday, May 28th, 1937, at 5.30

In German

SIEGFRIED

Siegfried	LAURITZ MELCHIOR
Der Wanderer	RUDOLF BOCKELMANN
Erda	EDITH FURMEDGE
Brünnhilde	KIRSTEN FLAGSTAD
Mime	ERICH ZIMMERMANN
Alberich	EUGEN FUCHS
Fafner	ROBERT EASTON
Der Waldvogel	STELLA ANDREVA

Conductor . Dr. WILHELM FURTWÄNGLER

Rosenfeld

Ingalill

Oslo   Unnamed pianist   78: Odeon (Scandinavia) 5348
1926   LP: Harvest H 1004
                                                                 Harvest states recorded 1924

Rossini

Stabat mater: Excerpt (Inflammatus)

March 1935   Orchestra   LP: Legendary LR 120
                      Unnamed conductor   CD: Legendary LRCD 1015

Schubert

Die Allmacht

London 1948	Unnamed pianist	LP: Anna ANNA 1016 LP: Legendary LR 120 CD: Legendary LRCD 1015
London April 1952	Moore, piano	78: HMV DB 21596 LP: EMI RLS 766

An die Musik

New York January 1953	McArthur, piano	LP: Victor LM 1738 LP: HMV ALP 1191

Am Grabe Anselmos

London March 1956	McArthur, piano	LP: Decca LXT 5263

Der Atlas

Stockholm 1949	Unnamed pianist	LP: Anna ANNA 1016 LP: Legendary LR 120 CD: Legendary LRCD 1015

Ave Maria

London March 1956	McArthur, piano	LP: Decca LXT 5263

Du bist die Ruh'

London April 1952	Moore, piano	78: HMV DB 21596

Der Erlkönig

London March 1956	McArthur, piano	LP: Decca LXT 5263

Die Forelle

New York March 1937	McArthur, piano	LP: Legendary LR 120 CD: Legendary LRCD 1015
London June 1937	McArthur, piano	78: HMV DA 1586 CD: Pearl GEMMCD 9092

Frühlingsglaube

London July 1952	Moore, piano	78: HMV DB 21554 LP: HMV HQM 1072 LP: EMI RLS 766

Ganymed

New York January 1953	McArthur, piano	LP: Victor LM 1738 LP: HMV ALP 1191

Im Abendrot

London June 1937	McArthur, piano	78: HMV DB 3305 78: Victor 15645
London July 1952	Moore, piano	78: HMV DB 21554

Die junge Nonne

London 1948	Unnamed pianist	LP: Anna ANNA 1016 LP: Legendary LR 120 CD: Legendary LRCD 1015
New York March 1953	McArthur, piano	LP: Victor LM 1870 LP: HMV ALP 1309

Die Krähe (Winterreise)

London 1948	Unnamed pianist	LP: Anna ANNA 1016

Lachen und Weinen

London June 1937	McArthur, piano	78: HMV DA 1586 CD: Pearl GEMMCD 9092

Die Liebe hat gelogen

New York March 1953	McArthur, piano	LP: Victor LM 1870 LP: HMV ALP 1309
London March 1956	McArthur, piano	LP: Rubini CC 1 Unpublished Decca recording

Des Mädchens Klage

London March 1956	McArthur, piano	LP: Decca LXT 5263

Die Post (Winterreise)

New York March 1953	McArthur, piano	LP: Victor LM 1870 LP: HMV ALP 1309

Der Musensohn

Stockholm 1949	Unnamed pianist	LP: Harvest H 1005 LP: Legendary LR 120 CD: Legendary LRCD 1015 Harvest incorrectly describes this song as Schubert (!!) Der Nussbaum

Der Tod und das Mädchen

London April 1952	Moore, piano	78: HMV DB 21596

Ueber allen Gipfeln (Wanderers Nachtlied II)

London May 1952	Moore, piano	LP: EMI RLS 766

Dem Unendlichen

London 1948	Unnamed pianist	LP: Anna ANNA 1016
London March 1956	McArthur, piano	LP: Decca LXT 5263

Der Wegweiser (Winterreise)

New York March 1953	McArthur, piano	LP: Victor LM 1870 LP: HMV ALP 1309

Schumann

Aus den östlichen Rosen (Myrthen)

Oslo
January 1955
Alme, piano
LP: Ed Smith UORC 243

Der arme Peter

Oslo
January 1955
Alme, piano
LP: Ed Smith UORC 243

Erstes Grün

London
March 1956
McArthur, piano
LP: Decca LXT 5263

Frauenliebe und -Leben, song cycle

New York
January 1953
McArthur, piano
LP: Victor LM 1738
LP: HMV ALP 1191

In der Fremde (Liederkreis)

London
March 1956
McArthur, piano
LP: Decca LXT 5263

Geduld (Myrthen)

Oslo
January 1955
Alme, piano
LP: Ed Smith UORC 243

Der Hans und die Grete

Oslo
January 1955
Alme, piano
LP: Ed Smith UORC 243

Der Himmel hat eine Träne geweinet

Oslo
January 1955
Alme, piano
LP: Ed Smith UORC 243

In meiner Brust

Oslo January 1955	Alme, piano	LP: Ed Smith UORC 243

Jasminenstrauch

Oslo January 1955	Alme, piano	LP: Ed Smith UORC 243

Liebeslied

Oslo January 1955	Alme, piano	LP: Ed Smith UORC 243
London March 1956	McArthur, piano	LP: Decca LXT 5263

Die Lotosblume (Myrthen)

London March 1956	McArthur, piano	LP: Decca LXT 5263

Meine Rose

Oslo January 1955	Alme, piano	LP: Ed Smith UORC 243
London March 1956	McArthur, piano	LP: Decca LXT 5263

Der Nussbaum (Myrthen)

London March 1956	McArthur, piano	LP: Decca LXT 5263

Die Soldatenbraut

London March 1956	McArthur, piano	LP: Decca LXT 5263

Widmung (Myrthen)

London March 1956	McArthur, piano	LP: Decca LXT 5263

Zum Schluss (Myrthen)

Oslo January 1955	Alme, piano	LP: Ed Smith UORC 243

Scott

Lullaby

Copenhagen July 1936	McArthur, piano	78: HMV DA 1512 78: Victor M 342 CD: Pearl GEMMCD 9092

Sibelius

Arioso

London February 1958	LSO Fjeldstad	LP: Decca LXT 5444/SXL 2030 LP: Decca BR 3059 LP: Decca ADD 248/SDD 248

Demanten pa marssnön

London February 1958	LSO Fjeldstad	LP: Decca LXT 5444/SXL 2030 LP: Decca ADD 248/SDD 248

Den första kyssen, orch. Fougstedt

London February 1958	LSO Fjeldstad	LP: Decca LXT 5444/SXL 2030 LP: Decca ADD 248/SDD 248

Flickan i fron sin älsklings möte, orch. Pingoud

London February 1958	LSO Fjeldstad	LP: Decca LXT 5444/SXL 2030 LP: Decca ADD 248/SDD 248

Höstkväll

London February 1958	LSO Fjeldstad	LP: Decca LXT 5444/SXL 2030 LP: Decca ADD 248/SDD 248

Kom nu hit, Död !

London	LSO	LP: Decca LXT 5444/SXL 2030
February 1958	Fjeldstad	LP: Decca BR 3059
		LP: Decca ADD 248/SDD 248

Men min fogel märks dock icke, orch. Pingoud

| London | LSO | LP: Decca LXT 5444/SXL 2030 |
| February 1958 | Fjeldstad | LP: Decca ADD 248/SDD 248 |

Om kvällen, orch. Jalas

| London | LSO | LP: Decca LXT 5444/SXL 2030 |
| February 1958 | Fjeldstad | LP: Decca ADD 248/SDD 248 |

Po verandan vid havet

| London | LSO | LP: Decca LXT 5444/SXL 2030 |
| February 1958 | Fjeldstad | LP: Decca ADD 248/SDD 248 |

Säf säf susa, orch. Hellmann

| London | LSO | LP: Decca LXT 5444/SXL 2030 |
| February 1958 | Fjeldstad | LP: Decca ADD 248/SDD 248 |

Se'n har jag ej frogat mera

| London | LSO | LP: Decca LXT 5444/SXL 2030 |
| February 1958 | Fjeldstad | LP: Decca ADD 248/SDD 248 |

Svarta rosor, orch. Pingoud

| London | LSO | LP: Decca LXT 5444/SXL 2030 |
| February 1958 | Fjeldstad | LP: Decca ADD 248/SDD 248 |

Var det en dröm, orch. Jalas

London	LSO	LP: Decca LXT 5444/SXL 2030
February 1958	Fjeldstad	LP: Decca BR 3059
		LP: Decca ADD 248/SDD 248

Vaaren flyktar hastigt

| London | LSO | LP: Decca LXT 5444/SXL 2030 |
| February 1958 | Fjeldstad | LP: Decca ADD 248/SDD 248 |

The Sibelius songs are sung in Swedish: it was to poems in that language that the vast majority of them were composed

Sinding

Den jomfru gik i Valmu-Vang

London McArthur, piano LP: Decca LXT 5327
November 1956 LP: Decca BR 3059.ECS 623

Der skreg en fugl

London McArthur, piano LP: Decca LXT 5327/ECS 623
November 1956

Eg tarv ikkje ljose aa kveikje

Oslo Alme, piano CD: Acanta 43.189
August 1958 Also published by Acanta on LP

Eg tykkjer det er reint langsamt

Oslo Alme, piano CD: Acanta 43.189
August 1958 Also published by Acanta on LP

Eg vil deg' kje elske

Oslo Alme, piano CD: Acanta 43.189
August 1958 Also published by Acanta on LP

Leit etter livet og liv det !

London McArthur, piano LP: Decca LXT 5327/ECS 623
November 1956

Mainat

Oslo F.Flagstad, piano 78: HMV (Scandinavia) X 1946
October 1923 LP: Harvest H 1004
  LP: Legendary LR 120
  CD: Legendary LRCD 1015
  CD: EMI CDH 763 3052

Sylvelin

London McArthur, piano LP: Decca LXT 5327
November 1956 LP: Decca BR 3059/ECS 623

Speaks

Morning

New York McArthur, piano LP: Victor LM 1738
January 1953 LP: HMV ALP 1191

Richard Strauss

Ach Lieb' ich muss nun scheiden

New York March 1953	McArthur, piano	LP: Victor LM 1870 LP: HMV ALP 1309

Allerseelen

London June 1936	McArthur, piano	78: HMV DA 1460 78: Victor 1726 CD: Pearl GEMMCD 9092
San Francisco October 1949	San Francisco SO Merola	LP: Rococo 5380 LP: Voce 98
New York March 1953	McArthur, piano	LP: Victor LM 1870 LP: HMV ALP 1309

Befreit

San Francisco October 1949	San Francisco SO Merola	LP: Rococo 5380 LP: Voce 98
London November 1956	McArthur, piano	LP: Decca LXT 5329/BR 3059

Beim Schlafengehen (4 letzte Lieder)

London May 1950	Philharmonia Furtwängler	LP: Ed Smith EJS 432 LP: Rococo 5380 LP: Cetra LO 501/FE 41/SLF 5011 LP: Turnabout THS 65116/TV 34830 CD: Palette PAL 1075 CD: Melodram CDM 25009 CD: Eklipse EKRCD 15 <u>Some versions incorrectly name</u> <u>orchestra as LPO and date as</u> <u>1949</u>
Berlin November 1952	Städtische Oper Orchestra Sebastian	LP: Melodram MEL 221 CD: Melodram MEL 26514 <u>Incorrectly dated May 1952</u>

Cäcilie

London June 1937	McArthur, piano	78: HMV DA 1587 78: Victor 1967
San Francisco October 1949	San Francisco SO Merola	LP: Rococo 5380 LP: Voce 98

Du meines Herzens Krönelein

New York March 1953	McArthur, piano	LP: Victor LM 1870 LP: HMV ALP 1309

Elektra: Excerpt (Orest! Orest!)

Berlin November 1952	Städtische Oper Orchestra Sebastian	LP: Rococo 5382 LP: Anna ANNA 1016 LP: Melodram MEL 221 LP: Legendary LR 120 CD: Melodram MEL 26514 CD: Legendary LRCD 1015 <u>Melodram incorrectly dated</u> <u>May 1952; some versions name</u> <u>orchestra as Berlin RIAS</u>

Frühling (4 letzte Lieder)

London May 1950	Philharmonia Furtwängler	LP: Ed Smith EJS 432 LP: Rococo 5380 LP: Cetra LO 501/FE 41/SLF 5011 LP: Turnabout THS 65116/TV 34830 CD: Palette PAL 1075 CD: Melodram CDM 25009 CD: Eklipse EKRCD 15 Some versions incorrectly name orchestra as LPO and date as 1949

Geduld

London November 1956	McArthur, piano	LP: Decca LXT 5329

Ich liebe dich

New York January 1953	McArthur, piano	LP: Victor LM 1738 LP: HMV ALP 1191

Ich trage meine Minne

London November 1956	McArthur, piano	LP: Decca LXT 5329

Im Abendrot (4 letzte Lieder)

London May 1950	Philharmonia Furtwängler	LP: Ed Smith EJS 432 LP: Rococo 5380 LP: Cetra LO 501/FE 41/SLF 5011 LP: Turnabout THS 65116/TV 34830 CD: Palette PAL 1075 CD: Melodram CDM 25009 CD: Eklipse EKRCD 15 Some versions incorrectly name orchestra as LPO and date as 1949
Berlin November 1952	Städtische Oper Orchestra Sebastian	LP: Melodram MEL 221 CD: Melodram MEL 26514 Incorrectly dated May 1952
Oslo January or May 1954	Alme, piano	LP: Ed Smith UORC 243 CD: Acanta 43.189 Also issued by Acanta on LP

Lob des Leidens

London November 1956	McArthur, piano	LP: Decca LXT 5329

Mein Herz ist stumm

New York April 1952	McArthur, piano	LP: Victor LM 2825

Mit deinen blauen Augen

London November 1956	McArthur, piano	LP: Decca LXT 5329

Ruhe, meine Seele

New York January 1953	McArthur, piano	LP: Victor LM 1738 LP: HMV ALP 1191

Seitdem dein Aug' in meines schaute

London November 1956	McArthur, piano	LP: Decca LXT 5329

September (4 letzte Lieder)

London May 1950	Philharmonia Furtwängler	LP: Ed Smith EJS 432 LP: Rococo 5380 LP: Cetra LO 501/FE 41/SLF 5011 LP: Turnabout THS 65116/TV 34830 CD: Palette PAL 1075 CD: Melodram CDM 25009 CD: Eklipse EKRCD 15 Some versions incorrectly name orchestra as LPO and date as 1949
Berlin November 1952	Städtische Oper Orchestra Sebastian	LP: Melodram MEL 221 CD: Melodram MEL 26514 Incorrectly dated May 1952

Wiegenlied

New York March 1953	McArthur, piano	LP: Victor LM 1870 LP: HMV ALP 1309

Zueignung

New York March 1953	McArthur, piano	LP: Victor LM 1870 LP: HMV ALP 1309

Thommesen

Vor sidste kveld

Oslo   Unnamed pianist   78: Odeon (Scandinavia) 5346
1926

Thomson

Kjaerlighet fra Gud, arr. Valen

Oslo   Fotland, organ   LP: Decca LXT 5662
September 1956   LP: Simax (Norway) PS 1801

Thrane

Aagots fjeldsang

Oslo   Unnamed pianist   78: Odeon (Scandinavia) 5332
1926   LP: Harvest H 1004
                                                 LP: Legendary LR 120
                                                 CD: Legendary LRCD 1015
                                                 <u>Harvest gives the improbable recording date of 1915</u>

Tyson

Sea moods

New York   McArthur, piano   LP: Victor LM 1870
March 1953   LP: HMV ALP 1309

Wagner

Der fliegende Holländer, abridged (1.Die Frist ist um; 2.Weit komm' ich her; 3.Summ' und brumm': 4.Traft ihr das Schiff im Meere an; 5.Mein Kind, du siehst mich auf der Schwelle: 6.Wie aus der Ferne; 7.Steuermann, lass' die Wacht; 8.Was muss ich hören?...to end)

London June 1937	Role of Senta Jarred, Lorenz, Janssen, Weber LPO Covent Garden Chorus Reiner	LP: Rococo 1008 LP: Discocorp RR 469 Traft ihr das Schiff LP: Ed Smith EJS 183 LP: Harvest H 1005 LP: Legendary LR 120 CD: Legendary LRCD 1015 CD: Memoir CDMOIR 403 Memoir also includes final scene of opera

Der fliegende Holländer: Excerpt (Traft ihr das Schiff im Meere an)

Havana 1948	Havana PO Krauss	CD: Eklipse EKRCD 15
San Francisco October 1949	San Francisco SO Merola	LP: Voce 98

Götterdämmerung

Milan April 1950	Role of Brünnhilde H.Konetzni, Höngen, Lorenz, J.Hermann, Pernerstorfer, Weber La Scala Orchestra and Chorus Furtwängler	LP: Ed Smith EJS 538 LP: Discocorp RR 420 LP: Murray Hill 940 477 LP: Everest S 476 LP: Cetra CFE 101/FE 40 CD: Cetra CDC 28/ECDC 100 CD: Cetra CDWFE 301/CDWFE 351 Excerpts LP: Rococo 5380 LP: Ed Smith EJS 318 CD: Cetra CDC 16
Oslo January and March 1956	Role of Brünnhilde Bjoner, Gustavson, Svanholm, Nordsjo, Johnsen, Grönneberg Oslo PO Norwegian Radio and Oslo Opera Choruses Fjeldstad	LP: Decca LXT 5205-5210 All of Brünnhilde's role LP: Decca GOM 579-580 Excerpts LP: Decca BR 3040

An unpublished Met broadcast may still survive: according to Metropolitan Opera Annals a live relay with Flagstad in the role of Brünnhilde took place on 12 May 1939

Götterdämmerung, Act 3

Rome May 1952	Role of Brünnhilde H.Konetzni, Suthaus, J.Hermann, Greindl RAI Rome Orchestra and Chorus Furtwängler	LP: Ed Smith EJS 318 LP: Cetra FE 20 Ed Smith incorrectly labelled Milan 1950

Götterdämmerung, unspecified extracts

London May 1936	Szantho, Melchior, Janssen, Weber LPO Covent Garden Chorus Beecham	HMV/Columbia Unpublished test pressings

Götterdämmerung: Excerpts (1.Zu neuen Taten; 2.Altgewohntes Geräusch..to end Act 1; 3.Heil dir Gunther...to end Act 2; 4.Her den Ring!...Starke Scheite)

London June 1937	Nezadal, Thorborg, Melchior, Weber, Janssen LPO Covent Garden Chorus Furtwängler	LP: Ed Smith EJS 431 LP: Japan JPL 1020-1022 LP: Discocorp RR 429 CD: Palette PAL 2007-2008 Starke Scheite only LP: Acanta 40.25520 CD: Memoir CDMOIR 403

Götterdämmerung: Excerpt (Zu neuen Taten, teurer Helde)

San Francisco November 1939	Melchior San Francisco Opera Orchestra McArthur	78: HMV DB 5885 78: Victor M 749 LP: Victor LM 2763 LP: RCA RB 6604 CD: RCA/BMG GD 87915
London June 1951 (14 June)	Svanholm Philharmonia Sebastian	LP: EMI EX 29 12273/29 10373 CD: EMI CMS 565 2122
London June 1951 (29 June)	Svanholm Philharmonia Weigert	HMV unpublished

Götterdämmerung: Excerpt (Helle Wehr! Heilige Waffe!)

London June 1951	Svanholm Philharmonia Weigert	LP: EMI EX 29 12273/29 10373 CD: EMI CMS 565 2122

Götterdämmerung: Excerpt (Starke Scheite schichtet mir dort)

Vienna September 1936	VPO Weingartner	LP: Teletheater 762.3589 CD: Koch Historic 3-1451-2
Philadelphia October 1937	Philadelphia Orchestra Ormandy	LP: RCA VIC 1517 LP: RCA PVM1-9068/AG 26.41399
San Francisco November 1939	San Francisco Opera Orchestra McArthur	78: HMV DB 6008 and 6011 78: Victor 15960 and 15963 CD: RCA/BMG GD 87915 CD: Nimbus NI 7847
London March 1948	Philharmonia Furtwängler	78: HMV DB 6792-6794/ DB 9323-9325 auto 78: Victor DM 644 45: Victor WHMV 1024 LP: Victor LHMV 1024 LP: Pathé FALP 119 LP: EMI 1C 147 01491-01492M LP: EMI 2C 051 03855/EX 29 12273 LP: French Furtwängler Society SWF 7803 LP: Toshiba WF 60024-60025 CD: Toshiba CE28-5590 CD: EMI CDH 763 0302/CMS 565 2122 Toshiba incorrectly dated 1952
Buenos Aires September 1948	Colón Orchestra Kleiber	CD: Pearl GEMMCD 9910
San Francisco 1949	San Francisco SO Merola	LP: Rococo 5382 LP: Voce 98
New York 1952	NYPO Walter	LP: Discocorp RR 531 CD: Nuova Era 2201 CD: Memories HR 4456-4457
London June 1952	Philharmonia Furtwängler	LP: HMV ALP 1016/HQM 1057 LP: Victor LHMV 1072 LP: Electrola E 90026/E 80954 LP: Seraphim 60003 LP: EMI 1C 147 01149M LP: Toshiba GR 2172/WF 60032 CD: Toshiba TOCE 6071 CD: EMI CHS 764 9352
Berlin November 1952	Städtische Oper Orchestra Sebastian	LP: Anna ANNA 1016 LP: Cetra LO 513 /Melodram MEL 221 CD: Hunt CD 576 CD: Melodram MEL 26514 Some issues incorrectly dated May 1952 or orchestra named RIAS
Bergen June 1953	Oslo Philharmonic Gruner-Hegge	CD: Eklipse EKRCD 15
New York March 1955	Symphony of the Air McArthur	LP: ERR 147 Orfeosonic SDST 3 LP: World Records T-366-367 CD: Music and Arts CD 263 Flagstad's final US appearance

Lohengrin

New York
March 1937

Role of Elsa
Branzell, Maison,
Huehn, L.Hofmann
Metropolitan
Orchestra & Chorus
Abravanel

CD: Walhall WHL 6
Excerpts
LP: Ed Smith UORC 194/EJS 183

Another Met broadcast may still survive: according to Metropolitan Opera Annals a live relay with Flagstad in the role of Elsa also took place on 19 February 1938

Lohengrin: Excerpt (Einsam in trüben Tagen)

New York
October 1935

Orchestra
Lange

78: HMV DB 2748
78: Victor 14181
LP: RCA VIC 1517/CAL 462
LP: Preiser LV 1372
CD: Nimbus NI 7847
CD: Pearl GEMMCD 9049/Pickwick GLRS 105

Vienna
May 1956

VPO
Knappertsbusch

45: Decca CEP 573
LP: Decca LXT 5249
LP: Decca LXT 6042/SXL 6042
LP: Decca ADD 212/SDD 212
LP: Decca ECS 826/GRV 11

Lohengrin: Excerpt (Euch Lüften, die mein Klagen)

Philadelphia
October 1937

Philadelphia
Orchestra
Ormandy

78: HMV DA 1623
78: Victor 1901
LP: RCA VIC 1517/CAL 462
LP: RCA PVM1-9068/AG 26.41399
LP: Preiser LV 1372
CD: RCA/BMG GD 87915
CD: Nimbus NI 7847/Pickwick GLRS 105

Lohengrin: Excerpt (Das süsse Lied verhallt)

New York
November 1940

Melchior
RCA Victor
Orchestra
McArthur

78: Victor DM 897
LP: Victor LCT 1105/LM 2618
LP: HMV ALP 1276
LP: RCA RB 6517/VIC 1681
CD: Memories HR 4456-4457

Parsifal

New York April 1938	Role of Kundry Melchior, Schorr, List, Cordon, Gabor Metropolitan Orchestra & Chorus Bodansky (Acts 1 & 3) Leinsdorf (Act 2)	LP: Ed Smith EJS 484

Parsifal, Act 2

London June 1951	Role of Kundry Lechleitner, O.Kraus Covent Garden Orchestra Rankl	LP: Ed Smith EJS 257 LP: Vocal Arts unnumbered CD: Legato LCD 144 Vocal Arts incorrectly described as Metropolitan Opera broadcast; both LPs have last 2 bars missing, but these are added from another recording on the CD

Parsifal: Extract (Dies alles hab' ich nun geträumt?...to end Act 2, including Ich sah das Kind)

New York November 1940	Melchior, Dilworth RCA Victor Orchestra McArthur	78: Victor M 755/DM 755 LP: Victor LCT 1105/LM 2763 LP: HMV ALP 1276 LP: RCA RB 6604/VIC 1681 LP: RCA (France) 731006-731010 CD: RCA/BMG GD 87915

Parsifal: Excerpt (Ich sah das Kind)

Vienna May 1956	VPO Knappertsbusch	45: Decca CEP 573 LP: Decca LXT 5249/LXT 5449 LP: Decca ADD 212/SDD 212 LP: Decca ECS 826/GRV 11 CD: Decca 414 6252

Das Rheingold

Vienna September and October 1958	<u>Role of Fricka</u> Watson, Madeira, Kuen, Kmennt, Svanholm, Wächter, Neidlinger, London, Kreppel, Böhme VPO Solti	LP: Decca LXT 5495-5497/ SXL 2101-2103/SET 382-384 LP: Decca 414 1011/414 1001 CD: Decca 414 1012/414 1002 <u>Excerpts</u> 45: Decca SEC 5042 LP: Decca LXT 5586/SXL 2230

Siegfried

New York January 1937	<u>Role of Brünnhilde</u> Andreva, Thorborg, Melchior, Laufkötter, Schorr, Habich, List Metropolitan Orchestra Bodansky	LP: Vocal Art unnumbered LP: Discocorp IGI 373
New York December 1938	<u>Role of Brünnhilde</u> C.Hartmann Metropolitan Orchestra Bodansky	Unpublished Metropolitan broadcast <u>Heil dir Sonne</u> LP: Ed Smith EJS 550
Milan March 1950	<u>Role of Brünnhilde</u> Moor, Höngen, Svanholm, Markwort, Weber, J.Hermann, Pernerstorfer La Scala Orchestra Furtwängler	LP: Ed Smith UORC 123 LP: Discocorp RR 420 LP: Murray Hill 940 477 LP: Everest S 477 LP: Cetra CFE 101/FE 39 CD: Cetra CDC 27 /ECDC 100 CD: Cetra CDWFE 301/CDWFE 351 <u>Heil dir Sonne</u> LP: Ed Smith EJS 390 CD: Cetra CDC 16

Siegfried: Excerpt (Heil dir Sonne! Heil dir Licht!)

London June 1951	Svanholm Philharmonia Sebastian	45: Victor WHMV 1024 LP: Victor LHMV 1024 LP: HMV BLP 1035/HQM 1138 LP: Seraphim 60082 LP: EMI 1C 047 01149M LP: EMI 1C 181 30669-30678M LP: EMI EX 29 12273/29 10373 CD: EMI CDH 763 0302/CMS 565 2122 <u>1C 181 30669-30678M and CDH 763 0302 begin only at "Dein war ich von je" and "Ewig war ich" respectively</u>

Tannhäuser

New York January 1936	Role of Elisabeth Fleischer, Halstead, Melchior, Tibbett, List, Gabor Metropolitan Orchestra & Chorus Bodansky	LP: Ed Smith

Other unpublished Met broadcasts may be preserved: according to
Metropolitan Opera Annals live relays with Flagstad in the role of
Elisabeth took place on 25 March and 16 December 1939 and on 4
January 1941

Tannhäuser: Excerpt (Dich teure Halle)

New York October 1935	Orchestra Lange	78: HMV DB 2748. 78: Victor 1418/8859 LP: RCA VIC 1208/VIC 1517 LP: RCA CAL 462 LP: Preiser LV 1372 CD: Nimbus NI 7847 CD: Pearl GEMMCD 9049/Pickwick GLRS 105
May 1938 Location not indicated	Unnamed pianist	LP: Ed Smith EJS 183 LP: Legendary LR 120 CD: Legendary LRCD 1015

Tannhäuser: Excerpt (Allmächtige Jungfrau)

New York October 1935	Orchestra Lange	78: HMV DB 2747 78: Victor 8920 LP: RCA VIC 1208/VIC 1517 LP: RCA CAL 462 LP: Preiser LV 1372 CD: Nimbus NI 7847 CD: Pearl GEMMCD 9049/Pickwick GLRS 105
London April 1948	Philharmonia Dobrowen	78: HMV DB 6795 45: Victor LP49-0783/12-1062 LP: EMI 1C 147 01491-01492M LP: EMI EX 29 02123 LP: EMI EX 29 10373 LP: EMI EX 29 12273 CD: EMI CDH 763 0302 CD: EMI CMS 764 0082

Tristan und Isolde

New York March 1935	Role of Isolde Branzell, Melchior, Schorr, L.Hofmann Metropolitan Orchestra & Chorus Bodansky	LP: Goldene Aera Richard Wagners GAW 301
London June 1936	Role of Isolde Kalter, Melchior, Janssen, List LPO Covent Garden Chorus Reiner	LP: Ed Smith EJS 465 LP: Discocorp RR 471 LP: Discoreale DR 10027-10030 CD: VAI Audio VAIA 1004 Act 1 complete and last two thirds of Act 3: CD: EMI CHS 764 0372 Original EMI CD issue incorrectly stated that this entire performance was conducted by Beecham
New York January 1937	Role of Isolde Thorborg, Melchior, Huehn, L.Hofmann Metropolitan Orchestra & Chorus Bodansky	LP: Ed Smith EJS 157
London June 1937 (18 June)	Role of Isolde Klose, Melchior, Janssen, S.Nilsson LPO Covent Garden Chorus Beecham	LP: Anna ANNA 1050 Act 1 LP: Ed Smith UORC 302 LP: Discocorp RR 223 Act 2 LP: Discocorp RR 223 CD: EMI CHS 764 0372 First third of Act 3 CD: EMI CHS 764 0372 Other excerpts LP: Ed Smith EJS 258 LP: Rococo 5382
London June 1937 (22 June)	Role of Isolde Branzell, Melchior, Schöffler, S.Nilsson LPO Covent Garden Chorus Beecham	Act 1 Unpublished test pressings Act 2 LP: Anna ANNA 1051 LP: Discocorp RR 223 Act 3 LP: Discocorp RR 223

Tristan und Isolde/continued

New York January 1938	Role of Isolde Wettergren, Melchior, Huehn, List Metropolitan Orchestra Bodansky	Unpublished Met broadcast Sink hernieder, Nacht der Liebe LP: Ed Smith EJS 258
New York March 1940	Role of Isolde Thorborg, Melchior, Huehn, List Metropolitan Orchestra & Chorus Leinsdorf	LP: Ed Smith UORC 182 CD: Music and Arts CD 647 Sink hernieder, Nacht der Liebe LP: Ed Smith UORC 159 UORC 182 incorrectly dated 1941; 2 brief extracts from this 1940 performance are also used to fill in gaps in the 1941 version as issued by Metropolitan Opera Guild (see below)
New York February 1941	Role of Isolde Thorborg, Melchior, Huehn, Kipnis Metropolitan Orchestra & Chorus Leinsdorf	LP: Metropolitan Opera Guild MET 3 LP: Melodram MEL 301 Tatest du's wirklich? LP: Acanta 40.23502
Buenos Aires August 1948	Ursuleac, Svanholm, Weber, Hotter Colón Orchestra Kleiber	Recording has been abridged but includes most of Isolde's part CD: Melodram MEL 25007 Sink hernieder, Nacht der Liebe LP: Rococo 5380
London June 1952	Role of Isolde Thebom, Suthaus, Fischer-Dieskau, Greindl Philharmonia Covent Garden Chorus Furtwängler	LP: HMV ALP 1030-1035 LP: Victor LM 6700 LP: Angel EL 3588 LP: HMV RLS 684 LP: EMI 1C 147 00899-00903M LP: EMI EX 29 06843/10 08993 CD: Toshiba CC30 3352-3355 CD: EMI CDS 747 3228 Excerpts 45: HMV 7EB 6018 LP: Victor LHMV 1072/LM 1829/LM 1909 LP: HMV HQM 1235/HLM 7026 LP: Seraphim 60145 LP: Electrola E 80712-80713 LP: EMI 1C 147 01491-01492M

Further unpublished Met broadcasts may be preserved: according to Metropolita Opera Annals live relays with Flagstad in the role of Isolde also took place on 8 February 1936, 18 February 1939 and 8 April 1939

A complete recorded performance with Flagstad as Isolde at La Scala Milan in 1951 (conducted by De Sabata) is mentioned by André Tubeuf; however, the singer that year was Grob-Prandl, and the only documentation of Flagstad in the role at La Scala is to be had from the extracts from 1947 and 1948 performances (see next page)

Flagstad

DE WAGNERVEREENIGING

STADSSCHOUWBURG - AMSTERDAM
ZONDAG 3 APRIL 1949 - AANVANG 1.30 UUR

Richard Wagner
TRISTAN UND ISOLDE

Muziekdrama in drie bedrijven

Tristan	Max Lorenz
Isolde	Kirsten Flagstad
Koning Marke	Sven Nilsson
Kurwenal	Hans Hotter
Brangäne	Constance Shacklock
Zeeman	John van Kesteren
Melot	Henk Noort
Herder	Wim Brüning
Stuurman	Guus Renaud

Scheepsvolk, ridders en schildknapen.

1e BEDRIJF
Op het dek van Tristan's schip tijdens de zeevaart van Ierland naar Cornwall

2e BEDRIJF
Op de burcht van koning Marke in Cornwall

3e BEDRIJF
Tristan's burcht in Bretagne

HET CONCERTGEBOUWORKEST

Dirigent: Erich Kleiber

Regie: Lothar Wallerstein — Decors: Emil Preetorius

A Truly Wonderful Recording

WAGNER
Tristan und Isolde

KIRSTEN FLAGSTAD
and **LUDWIG SUTHAUS**

with The Philharmonia Orchestra, and
Chorus of the Royal Opera House, Covent Garden,
conducted by

WILHELM FURTWÄNGLER

ALP1030-5

line-by-line libretto, 6/-.

HIS MASTER'S VOICE
LONG PLAY RECORDS

E.M.I. RECORDS LTD.

8-11 Great Castle Street, London, W.1.

Tristan und Isolde, miscellaneous excerpts (many fragmentary)

Milan February 1947	Cavelti, Beyron, Frantz, Schöffler La Scala Orchestra De Sabata	LP: Anna ANNA 1052 CD: Legendary LRCD 1025
Zürich June 1947	Cavelti, Lorenz, A. Böhm Tonhalle-Orchester Knappertsbusch	LP: Anna ANNA 1025
Milan April 1948	Anday, Lorenz, Weber, Schöffler La Scala Orchestra De Sabata	LP: Ed Smith UORC 260 <u>Liebestod</u> CD: Memoir CDMOIR 403

Tristan und Isolde, Act 1

London June 1950	Role of Isolde Shacklock, Svanholm, Schöffler Covent Garden Orchestra & Chorus Rankl	LP: Ed Smith UORC 228 Omits Prelude

Tristan und Isolde, Narration and Curse

London February 1947	LPO Rankl	LP: Anna ANNA 1025
London March 1948	Höngen Philharmonia Dobrowen	78: HMV DB 6748-6749 78: Victor DM 1435 45: Victor WDM 1435 LP: Victor LM 1151 LP: Electrola E 60619 LP: HMV HQM 1138 LP: Seraphim 60082/60619/IB 6158 LP: Toshiba GR 2192 LP: EMI 1C 147 01491-01492M LP: EMI EX 29 12273/29 10373 CD: EMI CDH 763 0302 <u>This version begins at</u> <u>Doch nun von Tristan?</u>
Berlin November 1952	Städtische Oper Orchestra Sebastian	LP: Anna ANNA 1016 LP: Cetra LO 513 LP: Melodram MEL 221 LP: Legendary LR 120 CD: Legendary LRCD 1015 CD: Hunt CD 576 CD: Melodram 26514 <u>Some issues incorrectly dated</u> <u>May 1952 and orchestra named</u> <u>as Berlin RIAS</u>

Tristan und Isolde, Act 2

San Francisco November 1937	Role of Isolde Meisle, Melchior, Huehn, List San Francisco Opera Orchestra Reiner	CD: Legato LCD 145
New York April 1939	Role of Isolde Szantho, Laholm, Gurney, Harris NYPO Barbirolli	LP: Roger Franck MR 2002 According to Jonathan Brown 37 bars from Lass meinen Liebsten ein are taken from another 1939 performance

Tristan und Isolde: Excerpt (Sink' hernieder, Nacht der Liebe)

San Francisco November 1939	Melchior San Francisco Opera Orchestra McArthur	78: HMV DB 5771-5772/6016-6017 78: Victor M 644/M 671/M 979 78: Victor AM 644/DM 644/DM 671/ DM 979 LP: Victor LM 2618/LM 6171 LP: RCA RB 6517/VIC 1618 CD: Metropolitan Opera MET 506 CD: RCA (USA) RG 79142 CD: Nimbus NI 7819 CD: Memories HR 4456-4457
London June 1949	Svanholm, Shacklock Philharmonia Böhm	78: HMV DB 21112-21114/ DB 9521-9523 auto 45: Victor WDM 1550 LP: Victor LM 1151 LP: Seraphim IB 6158 LP: EMI 1C 147 01491-01492M LP: EMI EX 29 12273/29 10373 CD: Testament SBT 1018 78 auto version may not have been published
San Francisco October 1949	Svanholm San Francisco SO Merola	LP: Ed Smith EJS 285 LP: Voce 98 CD: Eklipse EKRCD 15 This version proceeds only as far as Hold bewusster Wunsch; Eklipse incorrectly attributed to Havana 1948

Tristan und Isolde: Excerpt (Ich bin's, süssester Freund!)

Berlin November 1952	Städtische Oper Orchestra Sebastian	LP: Anna ANNA 1016 LP: Cetra LO 513 LP: Melodram MEL 221 CD: Hunt CD 576 CD: Melodram MEL 26514 Some versions incorrectly dated May 1952 and orchestra named as Berlin RIAS

Tristan und Isolde: Excerpt (Mild und leise)

New York October 1935	Orchestra Lange	78: HMV DB 2746 78: Victor 8859 LP: Victor LM 20144 LP: RCA VIC 1455/RL 85177 LP: Preiser LV 1372 CD: Musica Memoria MM 30283 CD: Nimbus NI 7847 CD: Pearl GEMMCD 9049/Pickwick GLRS 105 CD: RCA/BMG 09026 615802
San Francisco November 1939	San Francisco Opera Orchestra McArthur	78: HMV DB 6007 78: Victor M 644/DM 644 CD: RCA/BMG GD 87915
New York February 1949	NBC SO McArthur	LP: Legendary LR 120 CD: Legendary LRCD 1015
London April 1948	Philharmonia Dobrowen	LP: EMI EX 29 12273/29 10373 LP: Seraphim IB 6158 CD: EMI CDH 763 0302
Milan April 1948	La Scala Orchestra De Sabata	LP: Ed Smith UORC 260 LP: Rococo 5380
London August 1948	RPO Beecham	CD: Eklipse EKRCD 24
Havana 1948	Havana PO Krauss	CD: Eklipse EKRCD 15
San Francisco October 1949	San Francisco SO Merola	LP: Ed Smith EJS 285 LP: Voce 98
Berlin November 1952	Städtische Oper Orchestra Sebastian	LP: Anna ANNA 1016 LP: Cetra LO 513 LP: Melodram MEL 221 CD: Hunt CD 576 CD: Melodram MEL 26514 <u>Some versions incorrectly dated</u> <u>May 1952 and orchestra named as</u> <u>Berlin RIAS</u>
London December 1952	RPO Beecham	LP: Ed Smith EJS 399
Bergen June 1953	Oslo PO Gruner-Hegge	CD: Eklipse EKRCD 15
London October 1953	BBC SO Sargent	CD: Notes PGG 11019 CD: AS-Disc AS 360 CD: Memories HR 4456-4457
Oslo December 1953	Oslo PO Kielland	LP: Orpheum 8404
New York March 1955	Symphony of the Air McArthur	LP: ERR 142 LP: Orfeosonic SDST 3 LP: World Records T 366-367 CD: Music and Arts CD 263 <u>Flagstad's final US appearance</u>

Die Walküre

New York February 1935	Role of Sieglinde Kappel, Olszewska, Althouse, Schorr, List Metropolitan Orchestra Bodansky	Unpublished Met broadcast Act 1 only LP: Vocal Art unnumbered Flagstad's Metropolitan début
Milan March 1950	Role of Brünnhilde H.Konetzni, Höngen, Treptow, Frantz, Weber La Scala Orchestra Furtwängler	LP: Ed Smith EJS 534 LP: Discocorp RR 420 LP: Murray Hill 940 477 LP: Everest S 474 LP: Cetra LO 86/CFE 101/FE 38 CD: Cetra CDC 15/ECDC 100 CD: Cetra CDWFE 301/CDWFE 351 Excerpts LP: Ed Smith EJS 327 LP: Rococo 5380

Further unpublished Met broadcasts may still be preserved: according to Metropolitan Opera Annals live relays with Flagstad also took place on 18 December 1937 (role of Sieglinde) and on 17 February 1940 and 30 March 1940 (role of Brünnhilde)

Die Walküre, Act 1

Vienna October 1957	Role of Sieglinde Svanholm, Van Mill VPO Knappertsbusch	LP: Decca LXT 5429-5430? SXL 2074-2075 LP: Decca GOM 581-582/ GOS 581-582 LP: Decca GRV 26 CD: Decca 425 9632 Excerpts 45: Decca CEP 675/SEC 5074 LP: Decca (France) 7.660-7.661

Die Walküre: Excerpt (Der Männer Sippe)

New York March 1955	Symphony of the Air McArthur	LP: ERR 142 LP: Orfeosonic SDST 3 LP: World Records T 366-367 CD: Music and Arts CD 263 Flagstad's final US appearance Excerpt begins at Schläfst du Gast?
Vienna May 1956	VPO Knappertsbusch	LP: Decca LXT 5249 LP: Decca ADD 212/SDD 212 LP: Decca GRV 11

Die Walküre: Excerpt (Du bist der Lenz)

New York October 1937 (3 October)	Orchestra Iturbi	LP: Legendary LR 120 CD: Legendary LRCD 1015
Philadelphia October 1937 (17 October)	Philadelphia Orchestra Ormandy	78: HMV DA 1623 78: Victor 1901 LP: RCA VIC 1208/VIC 1617/CAL 462 LP: RCA PVM1-9068/AG 26.41399 LP: Preiser LV 1372 LP: EMI EX 29 01693 CD: RCA/BMG GD 87915 CD: Nimbus NI 7847 CD: Pearl GEMMCD 9049 CD: Pickwick GLRS 105 <u>Pearl edition is joined to form an entity with Melchior's almost contemporaneous version of Winterstürme</u>
New York March 1955	Symphony of the Air McArthur	LP: ERR 142 LP: Orfeosonic SDST 3 LP: World Records T 366-367 CD: Music and Arts CD 263 <u>Flagstad's final US appearance</u>
Vienna May 1956	VPO Knappertsbusch	LP: Decca LXT 5249 LP: Decca ADD 212/SDD 212 LP: Decca GRV 11

Die Walküre, Act 2

San Francisco November 1936	Role of Brünnhilde Lehmann, Meisle, Melchior, Schorr, List San Francisco Opera Orchestra Reiner	LP: Discocorp RR 426 LP: Edizione lirica EL 004 CD: Legato LCD 133 <u>LP editions have closing passage obliterated by radio announcer: this has been edited out on CD and replaced by Wotan's final words from another recording by Schorr</u>	

Die Walküre: Excerpt (Hojotoho! Hojotoho! Heiaha!)

New York   Orchestra   78: HMV DA 1460
October 1935   Lange   78: Victor 1726
                                     LP: RCA VIC 1517/CAL 462
                                     LP: Preiser LV 1372
                                     CD: RCA/BMG GD 87915
                                     CD: Nimbus NI 7847/NI 1430
                                     CD: Pickwick GLRS 105

New York   Orchestra   LP: Legendary LR 120
October 1938   Pelletier   CD: Legendary LRCD 1015

Die Walküre: Excerpt (Siegmund! Sieh' auf mich)

London   Svanholm   78: HMV DB 6962-6963
June 1949   Philharmonia   LP: Pathé FALP 119
                  Böhm   LP: Electrola E 60619
                                     LP: HMV HQM 1138
                                     LP: Seraphim 60082
                                     LP: EMI 1C 147 01491-01492M
                                     LP: EMI EX 29 12273/29 10373
                                     CD: Testament SBT 1018
                                     CD: EMI CMS 565 2122

Vienna   Svanholm   LP: Decca LXT 5389-5390/
May 1957   VPO   SXL 2031-2032
                  Solti   LP: Decca (France) 7.660-7.661

Die Walküre, Act 3

London   Role of Brünnhilde   LP: Ed Smith EJS 450
May 1937   Müller,   LP: Japan JPL 1020-1022
                  Bockelmann   LP: Discocorp RR 417
                  LPO   LP: Acanta 40.23520
                  Furtwängler   CD: Myto 91443/Acanta 44.1055
                                        Excerpts
                                        LP: Acanta BB 23119
                                        CD: Acanta 43.121
                                        CD: Palette PAL 2007-2008
                                        CD: Memoir CDMOIR 403

Vienna   Role of Brünnhilde   LP: Decca LXT 5389-5390/
May 1957   Schech, Edelmann   SXL 2031-2032
                  VPO   Excerpt
                  Solti   LP: Decca (France) 7.660-7.661

Der Engel (Wesendonk-Lieder)

London May 1948	Moore, piano	78: HMV DB 6841 LP: Electrola E 60809/WDLP 707 LP: Seraphim 60046 LP: EMI EX 29 12273 CD: EMI CDH 763 0302
London August 1948	RPO Beecham	LP: Rococo 5382 CD: Eklipse EKRCD 24 Rococo dated 1951
Havana 1948	Havana PO Krauss	CD: Eklipse EKRCD 15
Oslo December 1951 or December 1954	Oslo PO Fjeldstad	LP: Discocorp RR 531 LP: Acanta 40.23502 CD: Acanta 43.189
New York 1952	Walter, piano	LP: Discocorp RR 531
Berlin November 1952	Städtische Oper Orchestra Sebastian	LP: Melodram MEL 221 CD: Hunt CD 576 CD: Melodram MEL 26514 Some issues incorrectly dated May 1952 and orchestra named as Berlin RIAS
London October 1953	BBC SO Sargent	CD: AS-Disc AS 360 CD: Memories HR 4456-4457
New York March 1955	Symphony of the Air McArthur	LP: ERR 142 LP: Orfeosonic SDST 3 LP: World Records T 366-367 CD: Music and Arts CD 263 Flagstad's final US appearance
Vienna May 1956	VPO Knappertsbusch	LP: Decca LXT 5249/LW 5302 LP: Decca ADD 212/SDD 212 LP: Decca ECS 826/GRV 11 CD: Decca 414 6242

Im Treibhaus (Wesendonk-Lieder)

London May 1948	Moore, piano	78: HMV DB 6749 45: Victor WDM 1435 LP: Electrola E 60809/WDLP 707 LP: Seraphim 60046 LP: EMI EX 29 12273 CD: EMI CDH 763 0302
London August 1948	RPO Beecham	LP: Rococo 5382 CD: Eklipse EKRCD 24 Rococo dated 1951
Havana 1948	Havana PO Krauss	CD: Eklipse EKRCD 15
Oslo December 1951 or December 1954	Oslo PO Fjeldstad	LP: Discocorp RR 531 LP: Acanta 40.23502 CD: Acanta 43.189
New York 1952	Walter, piano	LP: Discocorp RR 531
Berlin November 1952	Städtische Oper Orchestra Sebastian	LP: Melodram MEL 221 CD: Hunt CD 576 CD: Melodram MEL 26514 Some issues incorrectly dated May 1952 and orchestra named as Berlin RIAS
London October 1953	BBC SO Sargent	CD: AS-Disc AS 360 CD: Memories HR 4456-4457
New York March 1955	Symphony of the Air McArthur	LP: ERR 142 LP: Orfeosonic SDST 3 LP: World Records T 366-367 CD: Music and Arts CD 263 Flagstad's final US appearance
Vienna May 1956	VPO Knappertsbusch	LP: Decca LXT 5249/LW 5302 LP: Decca LXT 6042/SXL 6042 LP: Decca ADD 212/SDD 212 LP: Decca ECS 826/GRV 11 CD: Decca 414 6242

Schmerzen (Wesendonk-Lieder)

London May 1948	Moore, piano	78: HMV DB 6842 LP: Electrola E 60809/WDLP 707 LP: Seraphim 60046 LP: EMI EX 29 12273 CD: EMI CDH 763 0302
London August 1948	RPO Beecham	LP: Rococo 5382 CD: Eklipse EKRCD 24 Rococo dated 1951
Havana 1948	Havana PO Krauss	CD: Eklipse EKRCD 15
Oslo December 1951 or December 1954	Oslo PO Fjeldstad	LP: Discocorp RR 531 LP: Acanta 40.23502 CD: Acanta 43.189
New York 1952	Walter, piano	LP: Discocorp RR 531
Berlin November 1952	Städtische Oper Orchestra Sebastian	LP: Melodram MEL 221 CD: Hunt CD 576 CD: Melodram MEL 26514 Some issues incorrectly dated May 1952 and orchestra named as Berlin RIAS
London October 1953	BBC SO Sargent	CD: AS-Disc AS 360 CD: Memories HR 4456-4457
New York March 1955	Symphony of the Air McArthur	LP: ERR 142 LP: Orfeosonic SDST 3 LP: World Records T 366-367 CD: Music and Arts CD 263 Flagstad's final US appearance
Vienna May 1956	VPO Knappertsbusch	LP: Decca LXT 5249/LW 5302 LP: Decca ADD 212/SDD 212 LP: Decca ECS 826/GRV 11 CD: Decca 414 6242

Stehe still (Wesendonk-Lieder)

Location/Date	Performers	Recordings
London May 1948	Moore, piano	78: HMV DB 6841 LP: Electrola E 60809/WDLP 707 LP: Seraphim 60046 LP: EMI EX 29 12273 CD: EMI CDH 763 0302
London August 1948	RPO Beecham	LP: Rococo 5382 CD: Eklipse EKRCD 24 Rococo dated 1951
Havana 1948	Havana PO Krauss	CD: Eklipse EKRCD 15
Oslo December 1951 or December 1954	Oslo PO Fjeldstad	LP: Discocorp RR 531 LP: Acanta 40.23502 CD: Acanta 43.189
New York 1952	Walter, piano	LP: Discocorp RR 531
Berlin November 1952	Städtische Oper Orchestra Sebastian	LP: Melodram MEL 221 CD: Hunt CD 576 CD: Melodram MEL 26514 Some issues incorrectly dated May 1952 and orchestra named as Berlin RIAS
London October 1953	BBC SO Sargent	CD: AS-Disc AS 360 CD: Memories HR 4456-4457
New York March 1955	Symphony of the Air McArthur	LP: ERR 142 LP: Orfeosonic SDST 3 LP: World Records T 366-367 CD: Music and Arts CD 263 Flagstad's final US appearance
Vienna May 1956	VPO Knappertsbusch	LP: Decca LXT 5249/LW 5302 LP: Decca ADD 212/SDD 212 LP: Decca ECS 826/GRV 11 CD: Decca 414 6242

Träume (Wesendonk-Lieder)

New York March 1937	Orchestra McArthur	LP: Legendary LR 120 CD: Legendary LRCD 1015
London May 1948	Moore, piano	78: HMV DB 6842 LP: Electrola E 60809/WDLP 707 LP: Seraphim 60046 LP: EMI EX 29 12273 CD: EMI CDH 763 0302
London August 1948	RPO Beecham	LP: Rococo 5382 CD: Eklipse EKRCD 24 <u>Rococo dated 1951</u>
Havana 1948	Havana PO Krauss	CD: Eklipse EKRCD 15
Oslo December 1951 or December 1954	Oslo PO Fjeldstad	LP: Discocorp RR 531 LP: Acanta 40.23502 CD: Acanta 43.189
New York 1952	Walter, piano	LP: Discocorp RR 531 CD: Memoir CDMOIR 403
Berlin November 1952	Städtische Oper Orchestra Sebastian	LP: Melodram MEL 221 CD: Hunt CD 576 CD: Melodram MEL 26514 <u>Some issues incorrectly dated</u> <u>May 1952 and orchestra named</u> <u>as Berlin RIAS</u>
London October 1953	BBC SO Sargent	CD: AS-Disc AS 360 CD: Memories HR 4456-4457
New York March 1955	Symphony of the Air McArthur	LP: ERR 142 LP: Orfeosonic SDST 3 LP: World Records T 366-367 CD: Music and Arts CD 263 <u>Flagstad's final US appearance</u>
Vienna May 1956	VPO Knappertsbusch	LP: Decca LXT 5249/LW 5302 LP: Decca LXT 6042/SXL 6042 LP: Decca ADD 212/SDD 212 LP: Decca ECS 826/GRV 11 CD: Decca 414 6242

Weber

Der Freischütz: Excerpt (Leise, leise)

London November 1938	Orchestra Unnamed conductor	LP: Ed Smith EJS 141 LP: Harvest H 1005 LP: Legendary LR 120 CD: Legendary LRCD 1015

Oberon: Excerpt (Ozean, du Ungeheuer)

Philadelphia October 1937	Philadelphia Orchestra Ormandy	78: HMV DB 3440 78: Victor 15224 LP: RCA VIC 1208/VIC 1517/CAL 462 LP: RCA PVM1-9068/AG 26.41399 LP: Preiser LV 1372 CD: Nimbus NI 7847 CD: Pickwick GLRS 105

Weyse

Gud signe vaart dyre fedreland, arr. Alnaes

Oslo September 1956	Fotland, organ	LP: Decca LXT 5662 LP: Simax (Norway) PS 1801

Winge

Kjaere lille gutten min

Oslo 1926	Unnamed pianist	78: Odeon (Scandinavia) 5552

Wolf

Anakreons Grab

London
November 1956

McArthur, piano

LP: Decca LXT 5329

Der Freund

London
November 1956

McArthur, piano

LP: Decca LXT 5329

Gebet

London
November 1956

McArthur, piano

LP: Decca LXT 5329

Gesang Weylas

London
November 1956

McArthur, piano

LP: Decca LXT 5329

Heb' auf dein blondes Haupt (Italienisches Liederbuch)

London
November 1956

McArthur, piano

LP: Decca LXT 5329

Morgenstimmung

London
November 1956

McArthur, piano

LP: Decca LXT 5329

Ueber Nacht

London
November 1956

McArthur, piano

LP: Decca LXT 5329

Zur Ruh'

London
November 1956

McArthur, piano

LP: Decca LXT 5329
LP: Decca BR 3059

Anonymous

Aa, Ola, Ola min eigen onge

Oslo 1926	Unnamed pianist	78: Odeon (Scandinavia) 5332 LP: Harvest H 1004 LP: Legendary LR 120 CD: Legendary LRCD 1015 Harvest dates this 1915!

Deilig er jordan, arr. Nielsen

Oslo September 1956	Fotland, organ	LP: Decca LXT 5662 LP: Simax (Norway) PS 1801

Eg ser deg ut for Glugjen

Oslo 1926	M.Flagstad, piano	78: Odeon (Scandinavia) 5373

Endnu et streif kun av sol

Oslo 1926	Unnamed pianist	78: Odeon (Scandinavia) 5371

Herre Gud, ditt dyre navn og aere, arr. Alnaes

Oslo September 1956	Fotland, organ	LP: Decca LXT 5662 LP: Simax (Norway) PS 1801

Jeg lagde mig saa sildig

Oslo 1926	M.Flagstad, piano	78: Odeon (Scandinavia) 5373

O come all ye faithful, arr. Woodgate

London April 1957	LPO Boult	45: Decca CEP 517/SEC 5002 LP: Decca LXT 5392/SXL 2049 LP: Decca ADD 207/SDD 207

Finnish National Anthem

New York 1939	Branzell, Melchior, Tibbett	LP: Ed Smith EJS 322 This is supposed to have been performed at a Finnish Relief Concert; the recording published as a Melchior 75th anniversary issue

Flagstad speaks

Very brief tribute to Ernestine Schumann-Heink

New York
December 1937

LP: Legendary LR 120
CD: Legendary LRCD 1015
This prefaces singing of Flagstad's Silent Night, Holy Night

Flagstad speaks of testing her voice, studying her roles and generally about her Wagnerian parts

BBC
London

LP: Rococo 5380
CD: Eklipse EKRCD 15

Desert Island Discs: entire spoken part of the programme, omitting the recordings chosen by Flagstad (interviewer Roy Plomley)

London
April 1952

CD: Eklipse EKRCD 15

Farewell speech after the final stage performance of Dido and Aeneas

London
October 1952

LP: Rococo 5380
LP: Legendary LR 120
CD: Legendary LRCD 1015
Incorrectly dated 1953

Flagstad (centre) in the role of Isolde

Astrid Varnay
born 1918

Discography compiled by John Hunt

Introduction

Which Wagnerian soprano holds the record of having twelve different portrayals of roles in Die Walküre preserved on published recordings ? The answer must be: Astrid Varnay.

In addition, there must be many singers who would prefer not to have their actual debut performance, their first appearance as a professional singer, preserved in a recording. However, that cannot apply to Astrid Varnay, called upon at the age of 23, at a few hours' notice, to replace Lotte Lehmann as Sieglinde in Die Walküre (New York, December 1941). On the same stage, only a week later, came an even more incredible debut as Brünnhilde in the same opera.

From then on Varnay was a Metropolitan Opera stalwart for 14 consecutive seasons, but it was inevitable that her origins (parents of Hungarian and Swedish birth respectively, and the musical tutelage of her husband Herman Weigert) should pull her back towards Europe.

This was the voice envisaged by Kirsten Flagstad as her legitimate successor, with its Nordic stamina and nobility of declamation, and it was in fact Flagstad's recommendation that brought Bayreuth its first post-war Brünnhilde, a role which Varnay (and, to a lesser extent, Mödl) monopolised until the arrival of Birgit Nilsson. For me personally this was the Wagnerian dramatic soprano before all others which supplemented rock-like strength with a more feminine flexibility (Walküre and Siegfried) and, when called for, outraged despair

(Götterdämmerung) to a far greater extent than her Swedish successor.

Whilst commercial recordings by Astrid Varnay are few, we possess an amazing wealth of recorded material capturing her in full flight. To hear her as Ortrud, as to have been there in the theatre, was a shattering experience, the very walls of the auditorium seemingly threatened by those Act 2 imprecations ! And the same applies to her Kundry and Kostelnicka (Janacek's Jenufa), other roles which I saw Varnay perform. I was lucky to have heard her in those parts which embody a troubled and daemonic undercurrent, a Varnay forte which emerged with ever increasing strength in the years of her maturity - though, heaven knows, it was already there in that neurotic and intense Senta of 1955 (Decca/Music and Arts). In that role alone she entirely eclipses both Flagstad and Nilsson !

As Wieland Wagner is reported to have said, "Why do I need real trees on my stage when I have an actress like Astrid Varnay ?"

John Hunt

Metropolitan OPERA HOUSE

GRAND OPERA SEASON 1941-1942
EDWARD JOHNSON General Manager
EDWARD ZIEGLER Assistant General Manager
EARLE R. LEWIS Assistant General Manager

SATURDAY AFTERNOON, DECEMBER 6, 1941, AT 2 O'CLOCK

DIE WALKUERE

Music Drama in Three Acts

BOOK and MUSIC by RICHARD WAGNER

Siegmund	Lauritz Melchior
Hunding	Alexander Kipnis
Wotan	Friedrich Schorr
Sieglinde	Lotte Lehmann
Bruennhilde	Helen Traubel
Fricka	Kerstin Thorborg

Valkyries:
- Helmwige .... Maria Van Delden (debut)
- Gerhilde .... Thelma Votipka
- Ortlinde .... Maxine Stellman
- Rossweisse .... Lucielle Browning
- Grimgerde .... Mary Van Kirk (debut)
- Waltraute .... Doris Doe
- Siegrune .... Helen Olheim
- Schwertleite .... Anna Kaskas

Conductor .... Erich Leinsdorf
Stage Manager .... Desire Defrere

POSITIVELY NO ENCORES ALLOWED

The Management requests the audience to abstain from applause at the fall of the curtain so long as the music continues.

SPECIAL NOTICE

MME. ASTRID VARNAY will make her debut this afternoon in "Die Walkuere" in the role of "Sieglinde," replacing MME. LOTTE LEHMANN, who is indisposed.

D'Albert

Tiefland

Düsseldorf June 1964	Role of Marta Green, Sauter, Hopf, Simonette, Ernster Deutsche Oper am Rhein Orchestra and Chorus Quennet	LP: Estro Armonico EA 059

Beethoven

Ah perfido!

Munich Date uncertain	Bavarian RO Weigert	45: DG EPL 30 091 LP: Austro-Mechanica 01.20216

Fidelio: Excerpt (Abscheulicher, wo eilst du hin?)

Vienna June 1951	Niederösterreich- isches Tonkünstlerorchester Weigert	LP: Remington RLP 199.45 LP: BASF 22.226453 LP: Acanta DE 22645 CD: Melodram MEL 16504

Brahms

Auf dem Kirchhofe

Munich 1954	Weigert, piano	CD: Myto MCD 90320

Mädchenlied

Munich 1954	Weigert, piano	CD: Myto MCD 90320

Cimara

Spiando ai vetri

Munich   Weigert, piano   CD: Myto MCD 90320
1954

De Banfield

Lord Byron's Love Letter, Excerpts

Rome   Role of Old Woman   LP: Victor LM 2258
ca. 1958   Ribla, Carruba,
                Carlin
                Academy SO
                Rescigno

Diémer

Le chevalier

Munich   Weigert, piano   CD: Myto MCD 90320
1954

Dvorak

Zigeunerlieder

Munich   Bender, piano   LP: Austro-Mechanica 01.20216
1961   Sung in German   CD: Myto MCD 90320

Fourdrain

L'Angelus

Munich   Weigert, piano   CD: Myto MCD 90320
1954

Giordano

Andrea Chenier

Walthamstow August 1982	Role of Contessa di Coigny Caballé, Kuhlmann, C.Ludwig, Pavarotti, Nucci, Krause WNO Chorus National PO Chailly	LP: Decca 410 1171 CD: Decca 410 1172

Grieg

Der gynger en baad paa boelge

Munich 1954	Weigert, piano Sung in German	CD: Myto MCD 90320/MCD 92466

En droem

Munich 1954	Weigert, piano Sung in German	CD: Myto MCD 90320/MCD 92466

En svane

Munich 1954	Weigert, piano Sung in German	CD: Myto MCD 90320/MCD 92466

Jeg elsker dig

Munich 1954	Weigert, piano Sung in German	CD: Myto MCD 90320/MCD 92466

FORTIETH SEASON

The Tuesday Morning Music Club

PRESENTS

ASTRID VARNAY, Soprano

Martin Rich *at the piano*

Program

I
Hear Ye, Israel! from "Elijah" ....*Mendelssohn*

II
Månljuset (Moonlight) ....*Jahn*
Fågeln (Birds) ....*Järnefelt*
Menuet d'Exaudet ....*Old French Bergeret*
Maman, dites-moi ....*Old French Bergeret*
Vieille Chanson ....*Bizet*

III
Aria — Ritorna Vincitor, from "Aida" ....*Verdi*

INTERMISSION

IV
Ungeduld ....*Schubert*
Heidenröslein ....*Schubert*
Mädchenlied ....*Brahms*
Vergebliches Ständchen ....*Brahms*

V
Love's Philosophy ....*Quilter*
When I have sung my songs ....*Charles*
So I go singing ....*Bransen*
Feast of Lanterns ....*Bantock*

VI
Aria — Dich, teure Halle, from "Tannhäuser" ......*Wagner*

MANAGEMENT: Haensel and Jones. Division Columbia
Concerts Corporation, 113 West 57th St., New York City

On November 18th, the program will be presented by
Florence Center, Cora Claiborne and Marion Jensen

WOMAN'S CLUB HOUSE
NOVEMBER 4, 1941

Saturday Evening, 24th February, 1968

The 14th performance at the Royal Opera House of

Jenůfa

Opera in three acts

Music by LEOŠ JANÁČEK
(By arrangement with Alfred A. Kalmus Ltd.)

Libretto drawn by the composer from the play by
Gabriela Preissová

English translation by
Edward Downes and Otakar Kraus

Conductor RAFAEL KUBELIK

Producer ANDE ANDERSON

Scenery and costumes by JAN BRAŽDA

THE COVENT GARDEN OPERA CHORUS
Chorus Master Douglas Robinson

THE COVENT GARDEN ORCHESTRA
Leader Charles Taylor

Characters in order of appearance

JENŮFA, step-daughter of the Kostelnička	MARIE COLLIER
GRANDMOTHER BURYJA, owner of the mill	ELIZABETH BAINBRIDGE
LACA KLEMEŇ, her step-grandson	RICHARD CASSILLY
JANO, a shepherd boy	VIVIEN TOWNLEY
BARENA, servant-girl in the mill	MARIA PELLEGRINI
FOREMAN of the mill	OTAKAR KRAUS
THE KOSTELNIČKA, widow, and daughter-in-law of Grandmother Buryja (Kostelnička means wife of the sexton or sacristan)	ASTRID VARNAY
WOMAN	ELIZABETH SHELLEY
STEVA BURYJA, grandson and heir of Grandmother Buryja, step-brother of Laca	JOHN LANIGAN
A MAID	MAUREEN MORELLE
MAYOR of the village	DAVID KELLY
HIS WIFE	JANET COSTER
KAROLKA, their daughter	PATRICIA REAKES
Musicians, Villagers, Recruits, Millhands and Village girls	

Halévy

La Juive: Excerpt (Il va venir)

Vienna June 1951	Niederösterreich- isches Tonkünstlerorchester Weigert	LP: Remington RLP 199.45 LP: BASF 22.226453 LP: Acanta DE 22645 CD: Melodram MEL 16504

Janacek

Jenufa

Munich March 1970	Role of Kostelnicka Hillebrecht, Benningsen, Cox, Cochran Bavarian State Opera Orchestra & Chorus Kubelik Sung in German	CD: Myto MCD 90422
Vienna October 1972	Role of Kostelnicka Jurinac, Rössel-Majdan, Cox, Cochran Vienna Opera Chorus VPO Kulka Sung in German	LP: Estro Armonico EA 061

Another performance may be preserved, as a Metropolitan opera broadcast with Varnay in the role of Kostelnicka took place in November 1974

Jenufa: Excerpts (A tak bychom sli celyin zivotemi; Necham jeste dvere otevreny; Ba ta tvoje okenicka uz pres; Co chvila, co chvila; Jenufko, ty jsi jeste vzhuru?; Tot' zrovna jde; Jeste jsem tu ja?; Vstante, pestounko moja)

London February 1968	Role of Kostelnicka Collier, Bainbridge, Cassily, Lanigan Covent Garden Orchestra Kubelik Sung in English	CD: Myto MCD 90422

Mascagni

Cavalleria Rusticana

Munich 1954	Role of Santuzza Münch, Hopf, Pease Bavarian Radio Orchestra & Chorus Sawallisch Sung in German	LP: Melodram MEL 412
Watford August 1979	Role of Mamma Lucia Caballé, Hamari, Carreras, Manuguerra Ambrosian Chorus Philharmonia Muti	LP: EMI SLS 5187/EX 29 08113 CD: EMI CMS 763 6502 Excerpts CD: EMI CDM 763 9332

Cavalleria Rusticana: Excerpt (Voi lo sapete)

Vienna June 1951	Niederösterreich- isches Tonkünstlerorchester Weigert	LP: Remington RLP 199.53 LP: BASF 22.226453/BB 23119 LP: Acanta DE 22645 CD: Melodram MEL 16504

Massenet

Hérodiade: Excerpt (Il est doux, il est bon)

Vienna June 1951	Niederösterreich- isches Tonkünstlerorchester Weigert	LP: Remington RLP 199.53 LP: Melodram MEL 076 CD: Memories HR 4560-4561

Thaïs: Excerpt (Ah! Je suis seule...Dis-moi que je suis belle)

Vienna June 1951	Niederösterreich- isches Tonkünstlerorchester Weigert	LP: Remington RLP 199.45 LP: BASF 22.226453 LP: Acanta DE 22645

Orff

Oedipus der Tyrann

Munich ca. 1966	Role of Jokasta Stolze, Kohn, Engen, Nöcker Bavarian Radio Orchestra & Chorus Kubelik	LP: DG 2740 227 CD: DG 437 0292

Ponchielli

La Gioconda: Excerpt (Suicio!)

Mexico City 1948	Orchestra del Palacio de Bellas Artes Picco	LP: Melodram MEL 433
Vienna June 1951	Niederösterreich- isches Tonkünstlerorchester Weigert	LP: BASF 22.226453 LP: Acanta DE 22645 CD: Melodram MEL 16504
Munich 1954	Bavarian RO Weigert	LP: Melodram MEL 076 CD: Memories HR 4560-4561

La Gioconda: Excerpt (Ecco, il velen di Laura/O furibondo iena/Addio, Gioconda!)

Mexico City 1948	Heidt, Baum Orchestra e Coro del Palacio de Bellas Artes Picco	LP: Melodram MEL 433

Puccini

Manon Lescaut: Excerpt (In quelle trine morbide)

Vienna June 1951	Niederösterreich- isches Tonkünstlerorchester Weigert	LP: Remington RLP 199.53 LP: Melodram MEL 076 CD: Memories HR 4560-4561

Respighi

Deita silvane, 5 liriche musicale su parole di Antonio Rubini

Munich 1961	Bender, piano	LP: Austro-Mechanica 01.20216 CD: Myto MCD 90320

Schubert

Aufenthalt (Schwanengesang)

Munich 1954	Weigert, piano	CD: Myto MCD 90320

Das Lied im Grünen

Munich 1954	Weigert, piano	CD: Myto MCD 90320

Richard Strauss

Elektra

New York December 1949	Role of Elektra Jessner, Nikolaidi, Jagel, Janssen Metropolitan Orchestra & Chorus Mitropoulos	LP: Robin Hood RHR 5101-5102 LP: OTARC OTA 4
New York February 1952	Role of Elektra Wegner, Höngen, Svanholm, Schöffler Metropolitan Orchestra & Chorus Reiner	LP: SJS 704-705
Cologne August 1953	Role of Elektra Rysanek, R.Fischer, Melchert, Hotter WDR Orchestra and Chorus Kraus	LP: Melodram MEL 112 CD: Gala GL 100.512
Salzburg August 1964	Role of Elektra Hillebrecht, Mödl, King, Wächter Vienna Opera Chorus VPO Karajan	LP: Estro Armonico EA 044 LP: Melodram MEL 718 CD: Melodram MEL 27044 CD: Orfeo C298 922I Excerpts CD: Hunt CDKAR 213
Vienna April and June 1981	Role of Klytemnestra Rysanek, Ligendza, Beirer, Fischer-Dieskau Vienna Opera Chorus VPO Böhm	VHS Video: Decca 071 4003 Laserdisc: Decca 071 4001 Ich habe keine guten Nächte LP: Legendary LR 204

Elektra: Excerpt (Allein! Weh, ganz allein)

Vienna June 1951	Niederösterreich- isches Tonkünstlerorchester Weigert	LP: BASF 22.226453 LP: Acanta DE 22645 CD: Melodram MEL 16504
Cologne September 1959	WDR Orchestra Mitropoulos	LP: Estro Armonico EA 035 LP: Cetra DOC 13 CD: Hunt CD 581

Die Frau ohne Schatten

Munich September 1976	Role of Amme Bjoner, Nilsson, King, Kohn, Fischer-Dieskau Bavarian State Opera Orchestra & Chorus Sawallisch	CD: Legendary LRCD 1029 Also issued by Legendary on LP

Der Rosenkavalier

New York February 1953	Role of Marschallin Conner, Stevens, Brownlee, Koreh, Hayward Metropolitan Orchestra & Chorus Reiner	LP: Melodram MEL 441 Excerpts CD: Gala GL 100.512

Der Rosenkavalier: Excerpt (Da geht er hin...Die Zeit, die ist ein sonderbar' Ding)

Vienna June 1951	Niederösterreich- isches Tonkünstlerorchester Weigert	LP: BASF 22.226453 LP: Acanta DE 22645 CD: Melodram MEL 16504

Der Rosenkavalier: Excerpt (Da geht er hin...to end Act 1)

Cologne 1954	Töpper WDR Orchestra Kraus	LP: Melodram MEL 076

BAYERISCHE STAATSOPER
NATIONALTHEATER MÜNCHEN

Mittwoch, 29. September 1976

Wiederaufnahme

Die Frau ohne Schatten

Oper in drei Akten von Hugo von Hofmannsthal

Musik von

RICHARD STRAUSS

Musikalische Leitung: Wolfgang Sawallisch

In der Inszenierung von Oscar Fritz Schuh · Spielleitung: Wolf Busse

Bühnenbild und Kostüme: Jörg Zimmermann

Chöre: Wolfgang Baumgart

PERSONEN

Der Kaiser	James King
Die Kaiserin	Ingrid Bjoner
Die Amme	Astrid Varnay
Der Geisterbote	Karl Christian Kohn
Hüter der Schwelle	Ruth Falcon
Stimme eines Jünglings	Norbert Orth
Stimme des Falken	Antonie Fahberg
Stimme von oben	Gudrun Wewezow
Barak, der Färber	Dietrich Fischer-Dieskau
Sein Weib	Birgit Nilsson
Der Einäugige	Hermann Sapell
Der Einarmige } des Färbers Brüder	Karl Helm
Der Bucklige	Lorenz Fehenberger
Stimmen der Ungeborenen	Lotte Schädle, Gertrud Freedmann, Ruth Falcon, Gudrun Wewezow, Helena Jungwirth
	Raimund Grumbach
Die Stimmen der Wächter der Stadt	Hermann Sapell
	Hans Wilbrink
Erste Dienerin	Lotte Schädle
Zweite Dienerin	Gertrud Freedmann
Dritte Dienerin	Gudrun Wewezow

Ort der Handlung:
1. Akt Auf einer Terrasse über den kaiserlichen Gärten. Färberhaus
2. Akt Färberhaus. Wald vor dem Pavillon des Falkners. Färberhaus. Schlafgemach der Kaiserin. Färberhaus
3. Akt Unterirdischer Kerker. Geistertempel: Eingang. – Geistertempel: Inneres. Landschaft im Geisterreich

Das Bayerische Staatsorchester · Der Chor der Bayerischen Staatsoper

Solo-Violine: Ingo Sinnhoffer · Solo-Cello: Franz Amann · Glasharmonika: Bruno Hoffmann

Technische Leitung: Gero Zimmermann	Kostümgestaltung: Günter Berger
Bühne: Günter Costa	Masken: Rudolf Herbert
Beleuchtung: Ulrich Eckert	Inspektion: Horst Wruck
Tonregie: Dieter Behne	und Herbert Gurth

Anfertigung der Dekorationen und Kostüme: Eigene Werkstätten

Das Werk ist erschienen im Verlag Fürstner Ltd., London W 8, vertreten durch B. Schott's Söhne, Mainz

Anfang 18 Uhr   Pausen nach dem 1. und 2. Akt   Ende 22 Uhr

Salome

Munich 1953	Role of Salome Klose, Patzak, Braun Bavarian RO Weigert	LP: Estro Armonico EA 035 LP: Discocorp IGI 289
Munich July 1971	Role of Herodias Rysanek, Stolze, Fischer-Dieskau Bavarian State Opera Orchestra Leitner	LP: Legendary LR 204 CD: Melodram CDM 27098 Closing scene CD: HRE Records HRE 1005
Vienna March 1974	Role of Herodias Stratas, Beirer, Weikl VPO Böhm	VHS Video: Decca 072 1093 Laserdisc: Decca 072 1091

Another performance may be preserved, as a Metropolitan opera broadcast with Varnay in the role of Herodias took place in February 1977

Salome: Excerpt (Du wolltest mich nicht deinen Mund küssen lassen!)

Vienna 1951	Niederösterreich- isches Tonkünstlerorchester Weigert	LP: BASF 22.226453 LP: Acanta DE 22645

Schlagende Herzen

Munich 1954	Weigert, piano	CD: Myto MCD 90320

Winterweihe

Munich 1954	Weigert, piano	CD: Myto MCD 90320

Verdi

Aida: Excerpt (Ritorna vincitor)

Vienna June 1951	Niederösterreich- isches Tonkünstlerorchester Weigert	LP: Remington RLP 199.45 LP: BASF 22.226453 LP: Acanta DE 22645

Aida: Excerpt (A te grave cagion m'adduce)

Munich 1954	London Bavarian RO Weigert	LP: Melodram MEL 076 CD: Memories HR 4560-4561

Un Ballo in maschera: Excerpt (Ecco l'orrido campo)

Vienna June 1951	Niederösterreich- isches Tonkünstlerorchester Weigert	LP: Remington RLP 199.53
Munich 1954	Bavarian RO Weigert	LP: Melodram MEL 076 CD: Memories HR 4560-4561

Un Ballo in maschera: Excerpt (Morrò, ma prima in grazia)

Munich Date uncertain	Bavarian RO Weigert	45: DG EPL 30 490
Munich Date uncertain	Bavarian RO Weigert Sung in German	78: DG 9100 45: DG EPL 30 489

Don Carlo: Excerpt (O don fatale)

Vienna	Niederösterreich-	LP: BASF 22.226453
June 1951	isches	LP: Acanta DE 22645
	Tonkünstlerorchester	CD: Melodram MEL 16504
	Weigert	

La Forza del destino: Excerpt (Madre, pietosa Vergine)

Munich	Bavarian RO	LP: Melodram MEL 433
1954	Weigert	
	Sung in German	

La Forza del destino: Excerpt (Pace, pace mio Dio!)

Munich	Bavarian RO	45: DG EPL 30 490
Date uncertain	Weigert	
Munich	Bavarian RO	78: DG 9100
Date uncertain	Weigert	45: DG EPL 30 489
	Sung in German	

Macbeth

Florence May 1951	Role of Lady Macbeth Penno, Petrov, Sarri, Tajo Maggio Musicale Orchestra & Chorus Gui	LP: Melodram MEL 433 Excerpts CD: Myto MCD 92466 CD: Hunt CDMP 471

Macbeth: Excerpt (La luce langue)

Vienna June 1951	Niederösterreich- isches Tonkünstlerorchester Weigert	LP: BASF 22.226453 LP: Acanta DE 22645 CD: Melodram MEL 16504
Munich 1954	Bavarian RO Weigert	LP: Melodram MEL 076 CD: Memories HR 4560-4561

Simon Boccanegra

New York January 1950	Role of Amelia Tucker, Warren, Valdengo, Szekely Metropoloitan Orchestra & Chorus Stiedry	LP: Melodram MEL 037 Excerpts LP: Hope Records HOPE 203

Simon Boccanegra: Excerpt (Come in quest' ora bruna)

Vienna June 1951	Niederösterreich- isches Tonkünstlerorchester Weigert	LP: Remington RLP 199.45 LP: BASF 22.226453 LP: Acanta DE 22645 CD: Melodram MEL 16504

Simon Boccanegra: Excerpt (Dinne, perchè in quest' eremo....Figlia! A tal nome palpito)

New York ca. 1950	Warren RCA Victor Orchestra Cellini	LP: Victor LM 2453 LP: RCA PVM1-9048 LP: RCA (Germany) AG 26.41372

Il Trovatore: Excerpt (D'amor sull' ali rosee)

Vienna June 1951	Niederösterreich- isches Tonkünstlerorchester Weigert	LP: Remington RLP 199.45 LP: BASF 22.226453 LP: Acanta DE 22645 CD: Melodram MEL 16504

Wagner

Der fliegende Holländer

New York December 1950	Role of Senta Glaz, Svanholm, Hayward, Hotter, S.Nilsson Metropolitan Orchestra & Chorus Reiner	LP: Raritas OPR 5
Bayreuth July 1955	Role of Senta Schärtel, Traxel, Windgassen, Uhde, Weber Bayreuth Festival Orchestra & Chorus Knappertsbusch	LP: Discocorp IGI 319 LP: Cetra LO 51 LP: Melodram MEL 550 CD: Music and Arts CD 319 CD: Hunt CDLSMH 34021 Wie aus der Ferne LP: Melodram MEL 094
Bayreuth August 1955	Role of Senta Schärtel, Traxel, Lustig, Uhde, Weber Bayreuth Festival Orchestra & Chorus Keilberth	LP: Decca LXT 5150-5152 LP: Decca D97 D3 Also issued on Decca Eclipse LP Excerpts LP: Telefunken BLK 16513
Bayreuth July 1956	Role of Senta Schärtel, Traxel, Cox, London, Van Mill Bayreuth Festival Orchestra & Chorus Keilberth	LP: Melodram MEL 560 CD: Myto MCD 93175

Der fliegende Holländer: Excerpts (Wie aus der Ferne..to end Act 2; Verloren ach Verloren!...to end of opera)

Bayreuth August 1956	Traxel, Weber, Schöffler Bayreuth Festival Orchestra Keilberth	LP: Melodram MEL 560

Der fliegende Holländer: Excerpt (Traft ihr das Schiff im Meere an)

Vienna June 1951	Niederösterreich- isches Tonkünstlerorchester Weigert	LP: Remington RLP 199.53/ RLP 199.137
Saarbrücken 1954	Saarland SO Michl	LP: Melodram MEL 076 CD: Memories HR 4560-4561

Götterdämmerung

Bayreuth August 1951 (4 August)	Role of Brünnhilde Mödl, Höngen, Schwarzkopf, Aldenhoff, Uhde, Weber, Pflanzl Bayreuth Festival Orchestra & Chorus Knappertsbusch	Decca unpublished
Bayreuth August 1951 (15 August)	Role of Brünnhilde Mödl, Siewert, Schwarzkopf, Aldenhoff, Uhde, Weber, Pflanzl Bayreuth Festival Orchestra & Chorus Karajan	Columbia unpublished
Bayreuth August 1952	Role of Brünnhilde Mödl, Siewert, Lorenz, Uhde, Greindl, Neidlinger Bayreuth Festival Orchestra & Chorus Keilberth	LP: Melodram MEL 529 CD: Paragon PCD 84025-84028
Bayreuth August 1953	Role of Brünnhilde Hinsch-Gröndahl, Malaniuk, Windgassen, Uhde, Greindl, Neidlinger Bayreuth Festival Orchestra & Chorus Krauss	LP: Foyer FO 1011 CD: Foyer 4CF 2010/15CF 2011 CD: Rodolphe RPC 32503-32509 Starke Scheite CD: Memories HR 4560-4561
Bayreuth August 1955	Roles of Brünnhilde and Third Norn Brouwenstijn, Ilosvay, Windgassen, Uhde, Greindl, Neidlinger Bayreuth Festival Orchestra & Chorus Keilberth	Decca unpublished
Bayreuth August 1956	Role of Brünnhilde Brouwenstijn, Madeira, Windgassen, Uhde, Greindl, Neidlinger Bayreuth Festival Orchestra & Chorus Knappertsbusch	LP: Melodram MEL 569 CD: Seven Seas (Japan) KICC 2274-2288 Zu neuen Taten & Starke Scheite CD: Music and Arts CD 319

Götterdämmerung/continued

Bayreuth August 1957	Role of Brünnhilde Grümmer, Ilosvay, Windgassen, Uhde, Greindl, Neidlinger Bayreuth Festival Orchestra & Chorus Knappertsbusch	LP: Estro Armonico EA 034 LP: Discocorp IGI 292 LP: Cetra LO 61/DOC 50 LP: Melodram MEL 579 CD: Music and Arts CD 256 CD: Laudis LCD 44013/154 020
Bayreuth July 1958	Role of Brünnhilde Grümmer, Madeira, Windgassen, Wiener, Greindl, Andersson Bayreuth Festival Orchestra & Chorus Knappertsbusch	LP: Melodram MEL 589 CD: Hunt CDLSMH 34044

Götterdämmerung: Excerpt (Zu neuen Taten)

Munich September 1955	Windgassen Bavarian RO L.Ludwig	LP: DG LPEM 19 063 CD: DG 423 7202

Götterdämmerung: Excerpt (Starke Scheite schichtet mir dort)

Munich June 1954	Bavarian RO Weigert	LP: DG LPEM 19 045/478 127 LP: DG 2721 111 CD: DG 423 7202

Lohengrin

New York January 1943	Role of Elsa Thorborg, Melchior, Sved, Cordon, Harrell Metropolitan Orchestra & Chorus Leinsdorf	LP: Ed Smith UORC 170 CD: Myto MCD 92466 Excerpts CD: Myto MCD 91341
New York January 1950	Role of Ortrud Traubel, Melchior, Janssen, Ernster, Guarrera Metropolitan Orchestra & Chorus Stiedry	LP: Danacord DACO 111-113 CD: Danacord DACOCD 322-324 Excerpt LP: Ed Smith UORC 158
Bayreuth August 1953	Role of Ortrud Steber, Windgassen, Uhde, Greindl, Braun Bayreuth Festival Orchestra & Chorus Keilberth	LP: Decca LXT 2880-2884 LP: Decca D12 D5 CD: Teldec 4509 936742 Excerpts LP: Telefunken BLK 16514/ LW 50512

Lohengrin/continued

Bayreuth August 1954	Role of Ortrud Nilsson, Windgassen, Uhde, Adam, Fischer-Dieskau Bayreuth Festival Orchestra & Chorus Jochum	LP: Cetra LO 77 LP: Melodram MEL 541 CD: Laudis LCD 44015 Excerpts LP: Gioielli della lirica GML 20 CD: Memories HR 4424-4425
Bayreuth July 1958	Role of Ortrud Rysanek, Konya, Blanc, Engen, Wächter Bayreuth Festival Orchestra & Chorus Cluytens	LP: Replica RPL 2489-2492 CD: Myto MCD 89062 Excerpts LP: Melodram MEL 085/MEL 590 CD: Melodram MEL 37073
Bayreuth August 1960	Role of Ortrud Nordmo-Loevberg, Windgassen, Adam, Neidlinger, Wächter Bayreuth Festival Orchestra & Chorus Maazel	LP: Melodram MEL 601
Bayreuth July and August 1962	Role of Ortrud Silja, J.Thomas, Vinay, Crass, Krause Bayreuth Festival Orchestra & Chorus Sawallisch	LP: Philips 6747 241
Milan March 1965	Role of Ortrud Bjoner, J.Thomas, Neidlinger, Crass, Krause Prague Theatre Chorus La Scala Orchestra Sawallisch	CD: Melodram MEL 37067

Lohengrin: Excerpt (Nun sei bedankt, mein lieber Schwan!..Mein Held! Mein Retter! Nimm' mich hin)

New York ca. 1950	Melchior, Janssen Columbia SO Leinsdorf	LP: Odyssey Y 31740

Varnay 145

BAYREUTHER FESTSPIELE
SONNTAG 21. AUGUST 1966
PARSIFAL · EIN BÜHNEN-
WEIHFESTSPIEL VON
RICHARD WAGNER

MUSIKALISCHE LEITUNG · PIERRE BOULEZ
REGIE UND INSZENIERUNG · WIELAND WAGNER
CHÖRE · WILHELM PITZ
SZENISCHE EINSTUDIERUNG · PETER LEHMANN
BELEUCHTUNGSEINRICHTUNG · PAUL EBERHARDT

PARSIFAL · SANDOR KONYA
KUNDRY · ASTRID VARNAY
AMFORTAS · THOMAS STEWART
GURNEMANZ · HANS HOTTER
KLINGSOR · GUSTAV NEIDLINGER
TITUREL · KURT BÖHME
GRALSRITTER · HERMANN WINKLER
GERD NIENSTEDT
KNAPPEN · RUTH HESSE / ELISABETH SCHÄRTEL
DIETER SLEMBECK / ERWIN WOHLFAHRT
KLINGSORS ZAUBERMÄDCHEN
ANJA SILJA / DOROTHEA SIEBERT
LILY SAUTER / RITA BARTOS
HELGA DERNESCH / SONA CERVENA
ALTSOLO · RUTH HESSE

TECHNISCHE LEITUNG · WALTER HUNEKE – BE-
LEUCHTUNG · KURT WINTER – MASKE · WILLI
KLOSE – AUSSTATTUNGSLEITUNG · JOACHIM STREU-
BEL – AUSSTATTUNGSASSISTENZ · WOLF MÜNZNER
REGIEASSISTENZ · RENATE EBERMANN / NIKOLAUS
LEHNHOFF / WOLFRAM DEHMEL / HENNING LO-
RENZ – MUSIKALISCHE ASSISTENZ · MAXIMILIAN
KOJETINSKY / ALFRED WALTER / HERBERT
VOCKS / JULIUS ASBECK / SIEGFRIED VÖLKEL

DER BEGINN JEDES AKTES WIRD 15 MINU-
TEN VORHER MIT EINER, 10 MINUTEN
VORHER MIT ZWEI UND 5 MINUTEN
VORHER MIT DREI FANFAREN ANGEKÜN-
DIGT · 1. AKT 16.00 UHR · 2. AKT 18.50 UHR
3. AKT 21.00 UHR · ENDE GEGEN 22.20 UHR
NACH BEGINN DER AKTE KEIN EINLASS

BAYREUTHER FESTSPIELE

SONNTAG, 29. JULI 1962

RICHARD WAGNER

DER RING DES NIBELUNGEN · EIN BÜHNENFESTSPIEL FÜR DREI TAGE UND EINEN VORABEND

ERSTER TAG: DIE WALKÜRE

SIEGMUND	FRITZ UHL	
HUNDING	GOTTLOB FRICK	
WOTAN	OTTO WIENER	
SIEGLINDE	JUTTA MEYFARTH	
BRÜNNHILDE	ASTRID VARNAY	
FRICKA	GRACE HOFFMAN	
GERHILDE	GERTRAUD HOPF	
ORTLINDE	ELISABETH SCHWARZENBERG	
WALTRAUTE	ANNI ARGY	
SCHWERTLEITE	ERIKA SCHUBERT	WALKÜREN
HELMWIGE	INGEBORG MOUSSA-FELDERER	
SIEGRUNE	GRACE HOFFMAN	
GRIMGERDE	SIEGLINDE WAGNER	
ROSSWEISSE	MARGARETE BENCE	

MUSIKALISCHE LEITUNG	RUDOLF KEMPE
REGIE UND INSZENIERUNG	WOLFGANG WAGNER
MUSIKALISCHE ASSISTENZ	PAUL ZELTER · WALTER BORN
REGIE-ASSISTENZ	ALFRED WALTER
KOSTÜM	MANFRED LINKE
MASKE	KURT PALM
AUSSTATTUNGSLEITUNG	WILLI KLOSE
PROJEKTIONEN	HANS-WOLFGANG DAHM
TECHNISCHE LEITUNG	REINHARD KRUMM
BELEUCHTUNG	JAKOB SCHLOSSTEIN

DER BEGINN DER AUFFÜHRUNG WIRD 15 MINUTEN VORHER MIT EINER FANFARE, 10 MINUTEN VORHER MIT ZWEI UND 5 MINUTEN VORHER MIT DREI FANFAREN ANGEKÜNDIGT
BEGINN 16.00 UHR · II. AUFZUG 18.15 UHR · III. AUFZUG 20.45 UHR · ENDE GEGEN 21.50 UHR · NACH BEGINN DER AUFZÜGE KEIN EINLASS

Lohengrin: Excerpt (Einsam in trüben Tagen)

New York January 1942	Orchestra Unnamed conductor	CD: International Record Collectors' Club CD 806 From a Radio Hour broadcast
New York April 1942	Orchestra Leinsdorf	78: Columbia (USA) 71399D LP: Columbia (USA) SL 19089 One of a group of 4 Wagner tracks which were Varnay's first studio recordings
London June 1951	Philharmonia Weigert	78: Columbia LX 1535 LP: EMI 1C 047 01373M
Vienna June 1951	Niederösterreich- isches Tonkünstlerorchester Weigert	LP: BASF 22.226453 LP: Acanta DE 22645 CD: Melodram MEL 16504 CD: Memories HR 4560-4561

Lohengrin: Excerpt (Euch Lüften, die mein Klagen)

New York April 1942	Orchestra Leinsdorf	78: Columbia (USA) 17354D LP: Columbia (USA) SL 19089 One of a group of 4 Wagner tracks which were Varnay's first studio recordings
Berlin 1953	Berlin RO Kraus	LP: Melodram MEL 076

Parsifal: Excerpt (Ich sah das Kind)

London June 1951	Philharmonia Weigert	78: Columbia LX 1560 LP: EMI 1C 047 01373M

Siegfried

Bayreuth August 1951 (2 August)	Role of Brünnhilde Lipp, Siewert, Aldenhoff, Kuen, S.Björling, Pflanzl, Dalberg Bayreuth Festival Orchestra Knappertsbusch	Decca unpublished
Bayreuth August 1951 (13 August)	Role of Brünnhilde Lipp, Siewert, Aldenhoff, Kuen, S.Björling, Pflanzl, Dalberg Bayreuth Festival Orchestra Karajan	LP: Melodram MEL 518 LP: Foyer FO 1004 CD: Melodram MEL 46106 CD: Hunt CDKAR 219
Bayreuth July 1952	Role of Brünnhilde Streich, Bugarinovic, Aldenhoff, Kuen, Hotter, Neidlinger, Böhme Bayreuth Festival Orchestra Keilberth	LP: Melodram MEL 528 CD: Paragon PCD 84021-84024
Bayreuth August 1953	Role of Brünnhilde Streich, Ilosvay, Windgassen, Kuen, Hotter, Neidlinger, Greindl Bayreuth Festival Orchestra Krauss	LP: Foyer FO 1010 CD: Foyer 4CF 2009/15CF 2011 CD: Rodolphe RPC 32503-32509
Bayreuth August 1955	Role of Brünnhilde Hollweg, Ilosvay, Windgassen, Kuen, Hotter, Neidlinger, Greindl, Bayreuth Festival Orchestra Keilberth	Decca unpublished
Bayreuth August 1956	Role of Brünnhilde Hollweg, Madeira, Windgassen, Kuen, Hotter, Neidlinger, Van Mill Bayreuth Festival Orchestra Knappertsbusch	CD: Seven Seas (Japan) KICC 2274-2288

Siegfried/continued

Bayreuth August 1957	Role of Brünnhilde Hollweg, Ilosvay, Aldenhoff, Kuen, Hotter, Neidlinger, Greindl Bayreuth Festival Orchestra Knappertsbusch	LP: Estro Armonico EA 033 LP: Discocorp IGI 292 LP: Cetra LO 60/DOC 49 LP: Melodram MEL 578 CD: Music and Arts CD 255 CD: Laudis LCD 44012/154 021
Bayreuth July 1958	Role of Brünnhilde Siebert, Ilosvay, Windgassen, Stolze, Hotter, Andersson, Greindl Bayreuth Festival Orchestra Knappertsbusch	LP: Melodram MEL 588 CD: Hunt CDLSMH 34043

Siegfried: Excerpt (Heil dir Sonne! Heil dir Licht!)

Munich June 1954	Windgassen Bavarian RO Weigert	LP: DG LPEM 19 045/478 127 LP: DG 2721 115 CD: DG 423 7202 2721 115 and 423 7202 begin at Ewig war ich

Tannhäuser

New York March 1948	Role of Venus Traubel, Stellman, Melchior, Janssen, Szekely Metropolitan Orchestra & Chorus Stiedry	CD: Myto MCD 93590
New York January 1955	Role of Elisabeth Krall, Thebom, Vinay, London, Hines Metropolitan Orchestra & Chorus Kempe	LP: Raritas OPR 409 LP: Melodram MEL 038

Tannhäuser: Excerpt (Dich teure Halle)

London June 1951	Philharmonia Sebastian	78: Columbia LX 1535 LP: EMI 1C 047 01373M LP: EMI EX 769 7411 CD: EMI CMS 769 7412
Vienna June 1951	Niederösterreich- isches Tonkünstlerorchester Weigert	LP: BASF 22.226453 LP: Acanta DE 22645 CD: Melodram MEL 16504
Munich 1954	Bavarian RO Weigert	LP: Melodram MEL 076 CD: Memories HR 4560-4561

Tannhäuser: Excerpt (Allmächtige Jungfrau)

New York April 1942	Orchestra Leinsdorf	78: Columbia (USA) 71399D LP: Columbia (USA) SL 19089 <u>One of a group of 4 Wagner</u> <u>tracks which were Varnay's</u> <u>first studio recordings</u>

Tristan und Isolde

Bayreuth July 1953	<u>Role of Isolde</u> Malaniuk, Vinay, Neidlinger, Weber Bayreuth Festival Orchestra & Chorus Jochum	LP: Documents OR 301 LP: Melodram MEL 535 CD: Hunt CDLSMH 34030

Tristan und Isolde: Excerpt (Weh, ach wehe! Dies zu dulden!)

Munich June 1954	Töpper Bavarian RO Weigert	LP: DG LPEM 19 018 LP: Decca (USA) DL 9897 LP: DG 2548 113 CD: DG 423 9552 <u>Original LP contained other</u> <u>excerpts (Querschnitt) not</u> <u>featuring Varnay</u>

Tristan und Isolde: Excerpt (Act 2 Prelude/Isolde! Geliebte! Tristan! Geliebter!)

Bamberg April 1959	Windgassen Bamberg SO Leitner	LP: DG LPEM 19 193/SLPEM 136 030

Tristan und Isolde: Excerpt (Sink' hernieder, Nacht der Liebe/Einsam wachend)

Chicago January 1953	Glaz, Vinay Chicago SO Reiner	LP: Raritas OPR 5
Bamberg April 1959	Töpper, Windgassen Bamberg SO Leitner	LP: DG LPEM 19 193/SLPEM 136 030 CD: DG 423 9552 <u>O sink hernieder</u> LP: DG 2538 058

Tristan und Isolde: Excerpt (Mild und leise)

London June 1951	Philharmonia Sebastian	78: Columbia LX 1417 LP: EMI 1C 047 01373M
Vienna June 1951	Niederösterreich- isches Tonkünstlerorchester Weigert	LP: BASF 22.226453 LP: Acanta DE 22645/40.23502 CD: Melodram MEL 16504
Munich October 1957	Bamberg SO Leitner	45: DG EPL 30 466 LP: DG LPEM 19 193/SLPEM 136 030 LP: DG 2548 113 CD: DG 423 9552

Die Walküre

New York December 1941	Role of Sieglinde Traubel, Thorborg, Melchior, Schorr, Kipnis Metropolitan Orchestra Leinsdorf	CD: Myto MCD 91341 Excerpts LP: Ed Smith EJS 543 Varnay's Metropolitan Opera début
Bayreuth August 1951 (1 August)	Role of Brünnhilde Rysanek, Höngen, Treptow, S.Björling, Van Mill Bayreuth Festival Orchestra Knappertsbusch	Decca unpublished

Bayreuth
August 1951
(12 August)
	Role of Brünnhilde
	Rysanek, H.Ludwig,
	Treptow, S.Björling,
	Van Mill
	Bayreuth Festival
	Orchestra
	Karajan
		Acts 1 and 2
		Columbia unpublished
		Act 3
		78: Columbia LX 1447-1454/
		    LX 8835-8842 auto
		LP: Columbia 33CX 1005-1006
		LP: Columbia (Germany)
		    C 90280-90281
		LP: EMI 1C 181 03035-03036M
		LP: Toshiba EAC 60215-60216
		CD: EMI CDH 764 7042
		Hier bin ich, Vater...dem
		freislichen Felsen zu nah'n!
		LP: EMI 1C 047 01373M

Bayreuth July 1952	Role of Brünnhilde Borkh, Malaniuk, Treptow, Hotter, Greindl Bayreuth Festival Orchestra Keilberth	LP: Melodram MEL 527 CD: Paragon PCD 84017-84020
Bayreuth August 1953	Role of Brünnhilde Resnik, Malaniuk, Vinay, Hotter, Greindl Bayreuth Festival Orchestra Krauss	LP: Foyer FO 1009 CD: Foyer 4CF 2008/15CF 2011 CD: Rodolphe RPC 32503-32509 Excerpts CD: Curcio-Hunt OPV 031

Die Walküre/continued

Bayreuth August 1954	Role of Brünnhilde Mödl, Milinkovic, Lorenz, Hotter, Greindl Bayreuth Festival Orchestra Keilberth	LP: Melodram MEL 547 CD: Melodram MEL 36102
Bayreuth July 1955	Role of Sieglinde Mödl, Milinkovic, Vinay, Hotter, Greindl Bayreuth Festival Orchestra Keilberth	LP: Melodram MEL 557
Bayreuth August 1955	Role of Brünnhilde Mödl, Milinkovic, Vinay, Hotter, Greindl Bayreuth Festival Orchestra Keilberth	Decca unpublished
Bayreuth August 1956	Role of Brünnhilde Brouwenstijn, Milinkovic, Windgassen, Hotter, Greindl Bayreuth Festival Orchestra Knappertsbusch	LP: Melodram MEL 567 CD: Seven Seas (Japan) KICC 2274-2288
Bayreuth August 1957	Role of Brünnhilde Nilsson, Milinkovic, Vinay, Hotter, Greindl Bayreuth Festival Orchestra Knappertsbusch	LP: Estro Armonico EA 032 LP: Discocorp IGI 292 LP: Cetra LO 59/DOC 48 LP: Melodram MEL 577 CD: Music and Arts CD 254 CD: Laudis LCD 44011/154 021
Bayreuth July 1958	Role of Brünnhilde Rysanek, Gorr, Vickers, Hotter, Greindl Bayreuth Festival Orchestra Knappertsbusch	LP: Melodram MEL 587 CD: Hunt CDLSMH 34042 Excerpts CD: Melodram MEL 37073
Bayreuth July 1960	Role of Brünnhilde Nordmo-Loevberg, Töpper, Windgassen, Hines, Frick Bayreuth Festival Orchestra Kempe	LP: Melodram MEL 607

Die Walküre: Excerpt (Der Männer Sippe)

Vienna June 1951	Niederösterreich- isches Tonkünstlerorchester Weigert	LP: Remington RPL 199.45/ RLP 199.137 LP: BASF 22.226453 LP: Acanta DE 22645

Die Walküre: Excerpt (Du bist der Lenz)

New York April 1942	Orchestra Leinsdorf	78: Columbia (USA) 17354D LP: Columbia (USA) SL 19089 LP: Odyssey 32 16 0304 <u>One of a group of 4 Wagner</u> <u>tracks which were Varnay's</u> <u>first studio recordings</u>
Vienna June 1951	Niederösterreich- isches Tonkünstlerorchester Weigert	LP: Melodram MEL 076 CD: Memories HR 4560-4561

Die Walküre: Excerpt (Siegmund, sieh' auf mich)

Munich September 1955	Windgassen Bavarian RO L.Ludwig	LP: DG LPEM 19 063 CD: DG 423 7202

Die Walküre: Excerpt (War es so schmählich?)

Munich 1954	G.London Bavarian RO Weigert	LP: Melodram MEL 076 CD: Memories HR 4560-4561

Der Engel (Wesendonk-Lieder)

Munich	Bavarian RO	LP: DG LPEM 19 059/2548 113
September 1955	L.Ludwig	CD: DG 423 9552

Im Treibhaus (Wesendonk-Lieder)

Munich	Bavarian RO	LP: DG LPEM 19 059/2548 113
September 1955	L.Ludwig	CD: DG 423 9552

Schmerzen (Wesendonk-Lieder)

Munich	Bavarian RO	45: DG EPL 30 459
September 1955	L.Ludwig	LP: DG LPEM 19 059/2548 113
		CD: DG 423 9552

Stehe still (Wesendonk-Lieder)

Munich	Bavarian RO	LP: DG LPEM 19 059/2548 113
September 1955	L.Ludwig	CD: DG 423 9552

Träume (Wesendonk-Lieder)

Munich	Bavarian RO	45: DG EPL 30 459
September 1955	L.Ludwig	LP: DG LPEM 19 059/2548 113
		CD: DG 423 9552

Dors, mon enfant

Munich	Bender, piano	LP: Austro Mechanica 01 20216
1961		CD: Myto MCD 90320

Attente

Munich	Bender, piano	LP: Austro Mechanica 01 20216
1961		

Mignonne

Munich	Bender, piano	LP: Austro Mechanica 01 20216
1961		

Weber

Der Freischütz: Excerpt (Und ob die Wolke)

Vienna June 1951	Niederösterreich- isches Tonkünstlerorchester Weigert	LP: Remington RPL 199.53 CD: Memories HR 4560-4561

Oberon: Excerpt (Ozean, du Ungeheuer)

Vienna June 1951	Niederösterreich- isches Tonkünstlerorchester Weigert	LP: Remington RLP 199.53 LP: Melodram MEL 076 CD: Memories HR 4560-4561

Weill

Aufstieg und Fall der Stadt Mahagonny

A performance of the opera may be preserved, as a Metropolitan opera broadcast with Varnay in the role of Begbick took place in November 1979

Wolf

Fussreise

Munich 1954	Weigert, piano	CD: Myto MCD 90320

Wolf-Ferrari

Quando di vidi

Munich 1954	Weigert, piano	CD: Myto MCD 90320

Letter of appreciation from Herbert von Karajan after Varnay's Salzburg appearance as Elektra

Martha Mödl
born 1912

Discography compiled by John Hunt

Introduction

Martha Mödl made her professional debut as a singer at the comparatively late age of 28. This was in the German industrial city of Remscheid, where she also worked in a munitions factory, operatic work becoming more difficult to find as German theatres were closing down under the pressure of wartime conditions.

From 1945 she was engaged by the Düsseldorf company as a high mezzo (or low soprano, as Mödl has sometimes described herself). Her parts included Dorabella, Carmen, Eboli and innumerable trouser roles like Cherubino, Hänsel and Oktavian. Her earliest (official) recordings for Telefunken included the main arias from Carmen and the Eboli aria "O don fatale" from Don Carlo. The former she considers in retrospect to be entirely bad and unrepresentative of her work at the time, whereas the Eboli scena can be said to be a fine example of German Verdi singing in a tradition which stretched back to the 1920s.

Martha Mödl's entry into the realm of dramatic soprano came when she was engaged by the conductor Joseph Keilberth for the part of Verdi's Lady Macbeth (again, we have a Telefunken recording of excerpts) and then by Hans Knappertsbusch for Bayreuth's first post-war Kundry. Mödl and her colleagues referred to him as "der grosse Hans", and accomodating herself to the long time-spans of the maestro was one of her most challenging and rewarding experiences, as was performing the same role, together with Leonore and Brünnhilde, a short time afterwards for Wilhelm Furtwängler. Both these conductors may have seemed, when viewed objectively, to have adopted notoriously slow tempi, but statistics do belie this, and the inspiration and tension which Mödl found in working with these men cannot be overlooked.

On the directorial side of opera Mödl's inspiration came from her work with Wieland Wagner both in Bayreuth and other houses, including the "Winter Bayreuth" of Stuttgart. It was an inspiration which derived primarily from the "stillness" of the music itself, restricting outward gestures and doing away with "pathos", and cultivating the same sparseness as was evident in Wieland's stage sets.

It was with the Stuttgart company that Martha Mödl visited London in Tristan und Isolde. Incidentally, some conductors still valued her great abilities as a mezzo, and she would have sung the role of Brangäne in Furtwängler's Furtwängler's HMV recording of Tristan had contractual problems with Wieland Wagner and Bayreuth not intervened.

Mödl was, like Gwyneth Jones later, not always a singer who respected her vocal limits when it came to dramatic involvement. Many such moments are to be encountered in the existing records of her Leonore and Brünnhilde, but such is the intensity of dramatic revelation that any blemishes are forgiven: to be convinced of this, hear only the "O namenlose Freude" duet from Fidelio with Wolfgang Windgassen. For comfortable listening one must go elsewhere !

The soprano was to return to her dramatic mezzo "Fach" once more when invited to sing the Götterdämmerung Waltraute at the 1966 and 1967 Bayreuth Festivals opposite the Brünnhilde of her great successor Birgit Nilsson. When questioned about this Mödl emphatically talks about "unsere Nachfolgerin", our successor, that is the successor of Mödl and Varnay, who were great friends and colleagues during their undisputed joint reign at Bayreuth for its first seven or eight seasons from 1951. Perhaps most fascinating of all among the many live archive performances available to collectors (first on LP, now on CD) is a 1954 Bayreuth Walküre with Mödl as Sieglinde and Varnay as Brünnhilde and the veteran Siegmund of Max Lorenz thrown in for good measure !

Mödl's work in contemporary opera constituted roles in Fortner's Bluthochzeit, Schoeck's Penthesilea, Orff's Antigonae, Reimann's Gespenstersonate, Stravinsky's Oedipus Rex and Henze's Elegie für junge Liebende. Only the Stravinsky and Henze are represented on record.

Her latter career, which continued well up to her 80th birthday in 1992, has embraced character mezzo parts like the Countess in Tchaikovsky's Pique Dame as well as a host of operetta and straight theatre roles. It is in fact likely that many operetta extracts with Martha Mödl exist in the archives of West German radio stations.

A final single representation of the singer on any Wagnerian shortlist will probably be her Kundry with Hans Knappertsbusch on Decca/Teldec and Melodram (who has captured the longing, or "Sehnen", of this role so well ?), although I am personally attracted to a sultry and vibrant rendering of the Wesendonk-Lieder (1955, conducted by Keilberth on Melodram LP). On the other hand, if I am using a recording to re-live a personal experience of the singer in the theatre, then it would have to be Mödl's menacing portrayal of Klytemnästra in Karajan's 1964 Salzburg Elektra (Melodram/Orfeo).

John Hunt

D'Albert

Tiefland: Excerpt (Ich weiss nicht, wer mein Vater war)

Hamburg	NDR Orchestra	LP: Melodram MEL 075
1951	Sanzogno	

Beethoven

Fidelio

Vienna October 1953	Role of Leonore Jurinac, Schock, Windgassen, Frick, Poell, Edelmann Vienna Opera Chorus VPO Furtwängler	LP: Replica RPL 2439-2441 LP: Cetra FE 8-10 CD: Cetra CDC 12 CD: Priceless D 20902
Vienna October 1953	Role of Leonore Jurinac, Schock, Windgassen, Frick, Poell, Edelmann Vienna Opera Chorus VPO Furtwängler	LP: HMV ALP 1130-1132 LP: Victor LHMV 700 LP: Electrola E 90071-90073 LP: HMV HQM 1109-1110 LP: EMI 1C 147 01105-01107M LP: EMI 2C 153 52540-52551 LP: Seraphim IC 6022 CD: Toshiba CE25 5819-5820 CD: EMI CHS 764 4962 Excerpts 45: HMV 7ER 5065/7ER 5069 45: Electrola E 50048/E 50566 LP: Electrola E 80038/SMVP 8029 LP: EMI 1C 047 00832
Vienna November 1955	Role of Leonore Seefried, Kmennt, Dermota, Weber, Schöffler, Kamann Vienna Opera Chorus VPO Böhm	LP: Melodram MEL 008 CD: Frequenz CMM 2 CD: Movimento musica 051.024

Fidelio: Excerpt (Abscheulicher! Wo eilst du hin?)

Berlin October 1952	Städtische Oper Orchestra Rother	LP: Telefunken TM 68003 LP: Telefunken BLE 14504/NT 539

Bizet

Carmen: Excerpt (L'amour est un oiseau rebelle)

Berlin	Städtische Oper	45: Telefunken UV 204
May 1962	Orchestra	LP: Telefunken BLE 14504/NT 539
	Rother	CD: Preiser 90136
	Sung in German	

Carmen: Excerpt (Près des remparts de Seville)

Berlin	Städtische Oper	45: Telefunken UV 204
July 1958	Orchestra	CD: Preiser 90136
	Rother	
	Sung in German	

Carmen: Excerpt (En vain, pour éviter les réponses amères)

Berlin	Städtische Oper	45: Telefunken UV 204
July 1958	Orchestra	CD: Preiser 90136
	Rother	
	Sung in German	

Brahms

Liebestreu

Berlin 1950	Raucheisen, piano	LP: Melodram MEL 075

Die Mainacht

Berlin 1950	Raucheisen, piano	LP: Melodram MEL 075

Der Schmied

Berlin 1950	Raucheisen, piano	LP: Melodram MEL 075

Wie Melodien zieht es mir

Berlin 1950	Raucheisen, piano	LP: Melodram MEL 075

Gluck

Alceste: Excerpt (Divinités du Styx)

Hamburg 1949	NDR Orchestra Schmidt-Isserstedt Sung in German	LP: Melodram MEL 075

Orfeo ed Euridice: Excerpt (Che farò)

Berlin 1950	Berlin RO L.Ludwig Sung in German	LP: Melodram MEL 075
Berlin June 1951	Städtische Oper Orchestra Löwlein Sung in German	LP: Telefunken TM 68009 LP: Telefunken BLE 14504/NT 539

Handel

Giulio Cesare: Excerpt (V'adoro, pupille)

Berlin	Berlin RO	LP: Melodram MEL 075
Date uncertain	Schmidt-Isserstedt	
	Sung in German	

Rodelinda: Excerpt (Dove sei?)

Hamburg	NDR Orchestra	LP: Melodram MEL 075
1951	Sanzogno	

Henze

Elegie für junge Liebende, scenes

Berlin	Role of Gräfin Carolina	LP: DG SLPM 138 875
1965	Fischer-Dieskau	
	Berlin RO and	
	Deutsche Oper Orchestra	
	Henze	

Humperdinck

Hänsel und Gretel: Excerpt (Suse, liebe Suse)

Hamburg	Lore Hoffman	LP: Melodram MEL 075
1949	NDR Orchestra	
	Schüchter	

Mussorgsky

Boris Godunov: Excerpts (1.Skuchno Marinye, akh, kak skuchno!; 2.V polnoch.. v sadu...u fontana; 3. Dimitri! Marina!)

Hamburg October 1950	Schock, Fiedler NDR Orchestra and Chorus Schüchter Sung in German	LP: Melodram MEL 075 (1 and 3) LP: Acanta 40.23550 (2 and 3)

Offenbach

Les brigands

Cologne ca. 1980	Role of Duchess Szapo, Kruse, Altmeyer, Möller, Van Ree WDR Orchestra and Chorus P.Steinberg Sung in German	LP: RCA RL 30474

Le pont des soupirs: Excerpt

Berlin Date uncertain	Maus Berlin RO Unnamed conductor Sung in German	Unpublished radio broadcast

Orff

Antigonae: Excerpt (O Grab, O Brautbett)

Munich 1953	Bavarian RO Sawallisch	LP: Melodram MEL 075

Purcell

Dido and Aeneas: Excerpt (When I am laid)

Hamburg 1949	NDR Orchestra and Chorus Schmidt-Isserstedt Sung in German	LP: Melodram MEL 075

Rimsky-Korsakov

The Snow Maiden: Excerpt (Snegurochka, o chom, ditya moyo mol' by tvoi?)

Hamburg 1949	NDR Orchestra and Chorus Schüchter Sung in German	LP: Melodram MEL 075

Schoenberg

Erwartung, song to a poem by Dehmel

1948 Location uncertain	Franze, piano	LP: Melodram MEL 075

Johann Strauss

Der Zigeunerbaron

Stuttgart ca. 1979	Role of Czipra Shade, Perry, Jerusalem, Brohner, W.Brendel, Rebroff SDR Orchestra and Chorus Eichhorn	VHS Video: Taurus 883

Richard Strauss

Elektra

Florence May 1950	Role of Klytemnestra A.Konetzni, Ilitsch, Klarwein, Braun Maggio Musicale Orchestra & Chorus Mitropoulos	LP: Cetra CS 1209/CS 519-520 LP: Cetra LPO 2010/TRV 7 LP: Everest S 459 LP: Turnabout THS 65040-65041 CD: Cetra 9075.137 CD: Cetra CDO 4
Salzburg August 1964	Role of Klytemnestra Varnay, Hillebrecht, King, Wächter Vienna Opera Chorus VPO Karajan	LP: Estro Armonico EA 044 LP: Melodram MEL 718 CD: Melodram MEL 27044 CD: Orfeo C298 922I

Die Frau ohne Schatten

Munich November 1963	Role of Amme Bjoner, Borkh, J.Thomas, Hotter, Fischer-Dieskau Bavarian State Opera Orchestra & Chorus Keilberth	LP: DG LPM 18 911-18 914/ SLPM 138 911-138 914 LP: DG 2721 161 Excerpts LP: DG SLPEM 136 422

Die schweigsame Frau

Munich 1973	Role of Housekeeper Grist, Grobe, McDaniel, Moll, Kusche Bavarian State Chorus & Orchestra Sawallisch	Unpublished video recording

Cäcilie

Berlin 1950	Raucheisen, piano	LP: Melodram MEL 075

Die Georgine

Berlin 1950	Raucheisen, piano	LP: Melodram MEL 075

Stravinsky

Oedipus Rex

Cologne
1954

<u>Role of Jocasta</u>
Pears, Krebs,
Rehfuss, Rohr
Cocteau
WDR Orchestra
and Chorus
Stravinsky

LP: Philips A 01137 L
LP: Philips ABL 3054
LP: CBS 61131

Tchaikovsky

Pique Dame

Vienna
May 1992

<u>Role of Countess</u>
Freni, Atlantov,
Leiferkus, Chernov
Vienna Opera Chorus
VPO
Ozawa

Unpublished video recording

ELEKTRA

CHARACTERS IN ORDER OF APPEARANCE

FIVE MAIDS	ELIZABETH BAINBRIDGE
	MAUREEN GUY
	NOREEN BERRY
	ANNE EDWARDS
	ELIZABETH VAUGHAN
THE OVERSEER	PAULINE TINSLEY
ELEKTRA	AMY SHUARD
CHRYSOTHEMIS, *her sister*	MARIE COLLIER
KLYTEMNESTRA, *their mother*	MARTHA MÖDL
THE CONFIDANTE	PHYLLIS SIMONS
TRAINBEARER	LEAH ROBERTS
A YOUNG SERVANT	JOHN DOBSON
AN OLD SERVANT	CHARLES MORRIS
ORESTES, *brother of Elektra and Chrysothemis*	JOHN SHAW
ORESTES' TUTOR	DAVID KELLY
AEGISTHUS	JOHN LANIGAN

Servants of the Household

Covent Garden performance 7 April 1966

STUTTGART STATE OPERA

WEDNESDAY, 14 SEPTEMBER 1955
FRIDAY, 16 SEPTEMBER 1955

TRISTAN UND ISOLDE

Opera in three acts by Richard Wagner

Musical Director: FERDINAND LEITNER

ROYAL PHILHARMONIC ORCHESTRA
Leader: Arthur Leavins

Producer: Heinz Arnold Scenery and costumes: Helmut Koniarsky
Chorus Master: Heinz Mende Technical Director: Adolf Assmann

Tristan	Wolfgang Windgassen
King Mark	Otto von Rohr
Isolde	Martha Mödl
Kurwenal	Gustav Neidlinger
Melot	Gustav Grefe
Brangäne	Grace Hoffman
Shepherd	Alfred Pfeifle
Steersman	Alfred Wohlgemuth
Young Seaman	Josef Traxel

Sailors, Knights, Courtiers, Servants

Interval after the I and II Act

For ALFRED DELVAL

Associate Stage Director: .... John Wickham
(by Courtesy of the Directors of the Sadler's Wells Trust)
Assistant Stage Director: .... Edward Holton
Assistant Production Manager: .... Henry Roberts

Guest performances at London's Royal Festival Hall

Verdi

Un Ballo in maschera

Cologne February 1951	Role of Ulrica Wegner, Schlemm, Fehenberger, Fischer-Dieskau WDR Orchestra and Chorus Busch Sung in German	LP: Brüder-Busch-Gesellschaft 12PAL 4779-4784 CD: Gala GL 100.509 Also published on CD on the Eklipse label, where it is incorrectly described as a 1943 performance featuring the tenor Helge Rosvaenge
Hamburg 1966	Role of Ulrica Berthold, Peters, Konya, Constantin Philharmonisches Staatsorchester Hamburg Opera Chorus Sanzogno Sung in German	Unpublished video recording

Don Carlo: Excerpt (O don fatale!)

Berlin June 1951	Städtische Oper Orchestra Löwlein Sung in German	LP: Telefunken TM 68009 LP: Telefunken BLE 14504/NT 539 CD: Preiser 90136

La Forza del destino

Hamburg 1952	Role of Preziosilla Martinis, Schock, Metternich, Frick, Neidlinger NDR Orchestra and Chorus Schmidt-Isserstedt Sung in German	LP: Eurodisc 300.724.435 Rataplan! LP: Melodram MEL 075

Macbeth: Excerpt (La luce langue)

Berlin June 1951	Städtische Oper Orchestra Löwlein Sung in German	LP: Telefunken TM 68009 LP: Telefunken BLE 14504/NT 539 CD: Preiser 90136

Macbeth: Excerpt (Una macchia è qui tuttora!)

Berlin June 1951	Städtische Oper Orchestra Löwlein Sung in German	78: Telefunken E 3891 LP: Telefunken TM 68009 LP: Telefunken BLE 14504/NT 539 CD: Preiser 90136

Wagner

Götterdämmerung

Bayreuth August 1951 (4 August)	Roles of Gutrune and Third Norn Varnay, Schwarzkopf, Höngen, Aldenhoff, Uhde, Pflanzl, Weber Bayreuth Festival Orchestra & Chorus Knappertsbusch	Decca unpublished
Bayreuth August 1951 (15 August)	Roles of Gutrune and Third Norn Varnay, Schwarzkopf, Siewert, Aldenhoff, Uhde, Pflanzl, Weber Bayreuth Festival Orchestra & Chorus Karajan	Columbia unpublished
Bayreuth August 1952	Roles of Gutrune and Third Norn Varnay, Siewert, Lorenz, Uhde, Greindl, Neidlinger Bayreuth Festival Orchestra & Chorus Keilberth	LP: Melodram MEL 529 CD: Paragon PCD 84025-84028
Bayreuth August 1953	Role of Brünnhilde Hinsch-Grondahl, Malaniuk, Windgassen, Uhde, Greindl, Neidlinger Bayreuth Festival Orchestra & Chorus Keilberth	LP: Allegro-Elite 3138-3142 LP: Melodram MEL 539 Provenance of this recording not indicated by Allegro-Elite; performance not to be confused with the other Götterdämmerung recording from 1953 conducted by Krauss and with Varnay in the role of Brünnhilde
Rome November 1953	Role of Brünnhilde Jurinac, Klose, Suthaus, Poell, Greindl, Pernerstorfer RAI Rome Orchestra & Chorus Furtwängler	LP: MRF Records MRF 34 LP: EMI RLS 702/EX 29 06703 CD: EMI CZS 767 1232/ CZS 767 1362 CD: Hunt CDWFE 359

Götterdämmerung/continued

Bayreuth August 1955	Role of Brünnhilde Brouwenstijn, Ilosvay, Windgassen, Hotter, Greindl, Neidlinger Bayreuth Festival Orchestra & Chorus Keilberth	Decca unpublished
Bayreuth July and August 1967	Role of Waltraute Nilsson, Dvorakova, Windgassen, Stewart, Greindl, Neidlinger Bayreuth Festival Orchestra & Chorus Böhm	LP: Philips 6747 037/6747 049 CD: Philips 412 4882/420 3252

Götterdämmerung: Excerpt (Starke Scheite schichtet mir dort)

Berlin November 1954	Städtische Oper Orchestra Rother	LP: Telefunken LGX 66036 LP: Telefunken BLE 14504/NT 539 CD: Preiser 90136

Parsifal

Bayreuth August 1951	Role of Kundry Windgassen, London, Weber, Uhde, Van Mill Bayreuth Festival Orchestra & Chorus Knappertsbusch	LP: Decca LXT 2651-2656 LP: Decca GOM 504-508 CD: Teldec 9031.760472 Excerpts LP: Telefunken BLK 16505
Bayreuth July 1954	Role of Kundry Windgassen, Greindl, Hotter, Neidlinger, Adam Bayreuth Festival Chorus & Orchestra Knappertsbusch	CD: Seven Seas (Japan) KICC 2341-2344
Bayreuth July 1956	Role of Kundry Vinay, Greindl, Fischer-Dieskau, Hotter, Blankenheim Bayreuth Festival Orchestra & Chorus Knappertsbusch	LP: Cetra LO 79 LP: Melodram MEL 563 CD: Hunt CDLSMH 34035

Parsifal, opening, up to and including first scene of Amfortas (Recht so! Habt Dank!)

Bayreuth August 1959	Wächter, Hines Bayreuth Festival Orchestra Knappertsbusch	CD: Hunt CDKAR 219 <u>Inadvertently included in a performance conducted by Karajan in Vienna 1961, with singers named as Höngen, Wächter & Hotter</u>

Siegfried

Bayreuth August 1953	Role of Brünnhilde Streich, Ilosvay, Windgassen, Kuen, Hotter, Greindl, Neidlinger Bayreuth Festival Orchestra Keilberth	LP: Allegro-Elite 3133-3137 LP: Melodram MEL 538 Provenance of this recording not indicated by Allegro-Elite; performance not to be confused with the other Siegfried recording from 1953 conducted by Krauss and with Varnay in the role of Brünnhilde
Rome November 1953	Role of Brünnhilde Streich, Klose, Suthaus, Patzak, Frantz, Greindl, Pernerstorfer RAI Rome Orchestra Furtwängler	LP: MRF Records MRF 23 LP: EMI RLS 702/EX 29 06703 CD: EMI CZS 767 1232/ CZS 767 1312 CD: Hunt CDWFE 359
Bayreuth August 1955	Role of Brünnhilde Hollweg, Ilosvay, Windgassen, Kuen, Hotter, Greindl, Neidlinger Bayreuth Festival Orchestra Knappertsbusch	Decca unpublished

Another performance may be preserved, as a Metropolitan opera broadcast with Mödl in the role of Brünnhilde took place in February 1957

Tristan und Isolde

Bayreuth July 1952	Role of Isolde Malaniuk, Vinay, Hotter, Uhde, Weber Bayreuth Festival Orchestra & Chorus Karajan	LP: Discocorp IGI 291 LP: Cetra LO 47 LP: Foyer FO 1038 LP: Melodram MEL 525 CD: Hunt CD 528 Excerpts LP: Rodolphe RP 12704 LP: WG Records APE 1210/WG 30010 LP: Gioielli della lirica GML 8 LP: Joker SM 1350 LP: Poyer FO 1034 CD: Classical Collection CDCLC 6009

Tristan und Isolde: Excerpt (Weh, ach wehe! Dies zu dulden!)

Berlin   Blatter   LP: Telefunken LGX 66036
November 1954   Städtische Oper   LP: Telefunken KT 11037
                Orchestra
                Rother

Tristan und Isolde, Liebesnacht

Berlin   Blatter,   LP: Telefunken LGX 66004
November 1954   Windgassen   LP: Telefunken BLE 14502/GMA 15
                Städtische Oper   LP: Telefunken KT 11037
                Orchestra
                Rother

Tristan und Isolde: Excerpt (Mild und leise)

Berlin   Städtische Oper   78: Telefunken VSK 9021
October 1952   Orchestra   45: Telefunken UV 102
                Rother   LP: Telefunken TM 68003
                                      LP: Telefunken KT 11037
                                      CD: Preiser 90136

Die Walküre

Bayreuth July 1953	Role of Brünnhilde Resnik, Malaniuk, Vinay, Hotter, Greindl Bayreuth Festival Orchestra Keilberth	LP: Allegro-Elite 3128-3132 LP: Melodram MEL 537 <u>Provenance of this recording not indicated by Allegro-Elite; performance not to be confused with the other Walküre recording from 1953 conducted by Krauss and with Varnay in the role of Brünnhilde</u>
Rome October and November 1953	Role of Brünnhilde H.Konetzni, Cavelti, Windgassen, Frantz, Frick RAI Rome Orchestra Furtwängler	LP: MRF Records MRF 41 LP: EMI RLS 702/EX 29 06703 CD: EMI CZS 767 1232/ CZS 767 1272 CD: Hunt CDWFE 359
Bayreuth July 1954	Role of Sieglinde Varnay, Milinkovic, Lorenz, Hotter, Greindl Bayreuth Festival Orchestra Keilberth	LP: Melodram MEL 547 CD: Melodram MEL 36102
Vienna September and October 1954	Role of Brünnhilde Rysanek, Klose, Suthaus, Frantz, Frick VPO Furtwängler	LP: HMV ALP 1257-1261 LP: Electrola E 90100-90104 LP: HMV HQM 1019-1023 LP: EMI 1C 149 00675-00679M CD: Toshiba CE25 5825-5827 CD: EMI CHS 763 0452 Excerpts LP: Electrola E 80039 LP: EMI 1C 063 00830
Bayreuth July 1955	Role of Brünnhilde Varnay, Milinkovic, Vinay, Hotter, Greindl Bayreuth Festival Orchestra Keilberth	LP: Melodram MEL 557
Bayreuth August 1955	Role of Sieglinde Varnay, Milinkovic, Vinay, Hotter, Greindl Bayreuth Festival Orchestra Keilberth	Decca unpublished

Der Engel (Wesendonk-Lieder)

Cologne	WDR Orchestra	LP: Melodram MEL 075
1955	Keilberth	

Im Treibhaus (Wesendonk-Lieder)

Cologne	WDR Orchestra	LP: Melodram MEL 075
1955	Keilberth	

Schmerzen (Wesendonk-Lieder)

Cologne	WDR Orchestra	LP: Melodram MEL 075
1955	Keilberth	

Stehe still (Wesendonk-Lieder)

Cologne	WDR Orchestra	LP: Melodram MEL 075
1955	Keilberth	

Träume (Wesendonk-Lieder)

Cologne	WDR Orchestra	LP: Melodram MEL 075
1955	Keilberth	

Birgit Nilsson
born 1918

with valuable assistance from
Clifford Elkin and Malcolm Walker

Discography compiled by John Hunt

Introduction

A German colleague of Birgit Nilsson, in fact one of the other Wagnerians whose discography is included in this volume, refers to her as a "Jahrhundertstimme" (voice of the century), an assessment which will be denied by very few commentators. And certainly among the Wagner sopranos featured here, Nilsson was the one who was in the right place at the right time to be fully served by the record industry in its stereo LP. Although she made recordings for most major labels, it was as a Decca artist that Nilsson became almost a household name to be quoted in the same breath as Joan Sutherland and Luciano Pavarotti, not to mention her regular Decca conductor, Sir Georg Solti.

The roles with which Birgit Nilsson established herself on the world's major operatic stages are all represented in her official discography, and when we add the unofficial items we have duplicates which add that extra dimension of hearing the voice "in action" before an audience.

Like Varnay before her and Jones after her, Nilsson supplemented the German "core" of her repertoire (the major Wagner and Strauss parts) with a considerable number of Italian roles, first and foremost Lady Macbeth and Turandot (the two most suited to her temperamentally) but going on to embrace the likes of Tosca, Amelia and Minnie. She is heard performing these on record with that added silver gleam that a purely Italianate voice rarely musters (at least among modern sopranos).

It is essentially the recorded live performances which help me to recall the thrill of hearing Birgit Nilsson. For that reason her Brünnhilde under Böhm is preferable to the epoch-making one under Solti, just as the live Elektras and Turandots have a dimension lacking in the coldness of the studios.

Birgit Nilsson's hearty approach to her art, together with her positive sense of humour, must make her an ideal guide to aspiring students who attend the lessons and master classes which she has instigated since her retirement from singing.

John Hunt

BIRGIT NILSSON

die berühmte Wagner-Sängerin

als Brünnhilde in SIEGFRIED
mit Wolfgang Windgassen · Hans Hotter · Gerhard Stolze
Gustav Neidlinger · Kurt Böhme · Marga Höffgen · Joan Sutherland
Georg Solti / Wiener Philharmoniker
5-30 LXT 2061/65-C — Stereo SXL 20 061/65-B Decca
Szenen aus dieser Oper
30 BLK 20 533 — Stereo SXL 20 533-B Decca
Ausgezeichnet mit dem GRAND PRIX DU DISQUE

als Isolde in TRISTAN UND ISOLDE
mit Fritz Uhl · Regina Resnik · Tom Krause · Arnold van Mill u. a.
Georg Solti / Wiener Philharmoniker
5-30 LXT 2026/30-C — Stereo SXL 20 026/30-B Decca
Szenen aus dieser Oper
30 BLK 20 505 — Stereo SXL 20 505-B Decca
Ausgezeichnet mit dem GRAND PRIX DU DISQUE

als Brünnhilde in DIE WALKÜRE
mit George London · Jon Vickers · Gré Brouwenstijn · David Ward
Erich Leinsdorf / Londoner Symphonie-Orchester
5-30 LM 6706-1/5-C — Stereo LSC 6706-1/5-B RCA Victor
Szenen aus dieser Oper
30 LM 2692-C — Stereo LSC 2692-B RCA Victor

auf DECCA und RCA Victor - Schallplatten von Weltruf

TELDEC »Telefunken-Decca« Schallplatten-Gesellschaft mbH., Hamburg 19

Adam

O holy night

Stockholm August 1963	Leven, organ	45: Decca CEP 5517/SEC 5517
Stockholm February 1977	Bondeman, organ	LP: Swedish Society SLT 33256

Adams

The Holy City

Stockholm February 1977	Bondeman, organ	LP: Swedish Society SLT 33256

Bach

Ave Maria, arranged by Gounod

Stockholm August 1963	Leven, organ	45: Decca CEP 5517/SEC 5517 CD: Bluebell ABCD 3001
Stockholm February 1977	Bondeman, organ	LP: Swedish Society SLT 33256

Bartok

Bluebeard's Castle

Stockholm February 1953	Role of Judith Sönnerstedt Stockholm RO Fricsay Sung in German	LP: Swedish Radio SRLP 1377 A version on HRE 225, also sung in German with the same soloists but from Danish Radio in 1953 and conducted by Frissholm, is probably identical to the Stockholm performance

190 Nilsson

Beethoven

Ah perfido !

London May 1958	Philharmonia Wallberg	LP: Columbia 33CX 1629/SAX 2284 LP: EMI 1C 187 00786-00787 CD: EMI CDM 763 1082
London May 1963	Covent Garden Orchestra Downes	45: Decca CEP 5533/SEC 5533
Vienna 1971	VSO Leitner	LP: DG 2721 138/2721 206/2538 098

Egmont: Klärchen-Lieder (Die Trommel gerühret; Freudvoll und leidvoll)

London November 1957	Philharmonia Klemperer	45: Columbia SEL 1609 LP: Columbia 33CX 1575 LP: EMI ED 29 02531/EX 29 03793 CD: EMI CDC 747 1882/CDM 763 3582

Die Ehre Gottes aus der Natur

Stockholm February 1977	Bondeman, organ	LP: Swedish Society SLT 33256

Fidelio

Cologne
January 1956
<u>Role of Leonore</u>
Wenglor, Hopf,
Unger, Schöffler,
Frick, H.Braun
WDR Orchestra
and Chorus
Kleiber
LP: Rococo 1014
LP: Cetra LO 68
CD: Hunt CDLSMH 34048

New York
February 1960
<u>Role of Leonore</u>
Hurley, Vickers,
Anthony, Tozzi,
Uhde, Czerwenka
Metropolitan
Orchestra & Chorus
Böhm
LP: Melodram MEL 045

Milan
December 1960
<u>Role of Leonore</u>
Lipp, Vickers,
Unger, Hotter,
Frick, Crass
La Scala Orchestra
and Chorus
Karajan
LP: HRE Records HRE 388

Fidelio/concluded

Vienna March and June 1964	Role of Leonore Sciutti, McCracken, Grobe, Krause, Böhme, Prey Vienna Opera Chorus VPO Maazel	LP: Decca MET 272-273/ SET 272-273 Abscheulicher CD: Decca 421 3232
Rome March 1970	Role of Leonore Donath, Spiess, Unger, Vogel, Crass RAI Rome Chorus and Orchestra Bernstein	CD: Hunt CDLSMH 34049

Other recordings of the opera may be preserved, as Metropolitan Opera broadcasts with Nilsson in the role of Leonore also took place in January 1963 and January 1966

Fidelio: Excerpt (Abscheulicher!)

London May 1958	Philharmonia Wallberg	LP: Columbia 33CX 1629/SAX 2284 LP: Angel 35715/60353 LP: EMI 1C 187 00786-00787 CD: EMI CDM 763 1082
Stockholm January 1961	Stockholm RO Grevillius	CD: Bluebell ABCD 055
London June 1963	Covent Garden Orchestra Downes	LP: Decca LXT 6077/SXL 6077

Missa Solemnis

Stockholm March 1948	Soprano soloist Tunnell, Bäckelin, S.Björling Stockholm Philharmonic Chorus & Orchestra Kleiber	LP: Discocorp IGI 366

Berwald

Estrella de Soria: Excerpt (Estrella's aria)

Stockholm April 1947	Stockholm RO Frykberg	CD: Bluebell ABCD 055 Earliest extant recording of Birgit Nilsson

Catalani

La Wally: Excerpt (Ebben? Ne andro lontana)

Sweden 1978-1979	Roos, piano	LP: Bluebell BELL 109

Coates

Bird songs at eventide

Sweden 1978-1979	Roos, piano	LP: Bluebell BELL 109

Eriksson

Stora och underbare äro dina verk

Stockholm February 1977	Bondeman, organ	LP: Swedish Society SLT 33256

Franck

Panis angelicus

Stockholm August 1963	Leven, organ	45: Decca CEP 5517/SEC 5517
Stockholm February 1977	Bondeman, organ	LP: Swedish Society SLT 33256

De Frumerie

När du sluter mina ögon

Stockholm September 1974	Parsons, piano	CD: Bluebell ABCD 009 Previously issued by Bluebell on LP

Som en väg

Stockholm September 1974	Parsons, piano	CD: Bluebell ABCD 009 Previously issued by Bluebell on LP

Gounod

O divine redeemer

Stockholm February 1977	Bondeman, organ Sung in Latin	LP: Swedish Society SLT 33256

Royal Festival Hall
Monday, September 28 1970 at 8:00 pm

Jenny Lind Memorial Concert

Birgit Nilsson

First recital performance by Miss Nilsson in this country

Programme

C. W. Gluck	Divinites du Styx (from "Alceste")
H. Wolf	Gebet
	Begegnung
	Kennst Du das Land (Lied der Mignon)
R. Strauss	Morgen
	Befreit
	Wiegenlied
	Zueignung

INTERVAL

J. Sibelius	Flickan kom ifran sin alsklings mote
	Var det en drom?
	Varen flyktar hastigt
T. Rangstrom	Flickan under nymanen
	Melodi
	Skoldmon
E. Grieg	Og jeg vil ha mig en hjertenskjaer
	En svane
	En drom

Encores
3 Scandinavian songs
Verdi — Pace pace (La Forza del destino)
Puccini — Vissi d'arte (Tosca)

Tickets at 63/- 42/- 30/- 21/- 15/-
from the Royal Festival Hall
Box Office 01-928 3191
Promoted by the Swedish Institute
for Cultural Relations
Management: Wilhelmina Hoedeman

Grieg

<u>Den store hvide flok</u>

Stockholm February 1977	Bondeman, organ	LP: Swedish Society SLT 33256

<u>En droem</u>

Stockholm September 1974	Parsons, piano	CD: Bluebell ABCD 009 <u>Previously issued by Bluebell on LP</u>
Sweden 1978-1979	Roos, piano	LP: Bluebell BELL 109

<u>En svane</u>

New York May 1961	Taubman, piano	LP: RCA LM 2578/LSC 2578 CD: RCA/BMG 09026 618792/ 09026 618272
Vienna April 1965	VPO Bokstedt	LP: Decca LXT 6185/SXL 6185
Stockholm September 1974	Parsons, piano	CD: Bluebell ABCD 009 <u>Previously issued by Bluebell on LP</u>

Et haab

Sweden   Roos, piano   LP: Bluebell BELL 114
1978-1979

Fra Monte Pincio

Vienna   VPO   LP: Decca LXT 6185/SXL 6185
April 1965   Bokstedt

Jeg elsker dig

New York   Taubman, piano   LP: RCA LM 2578/LSC 2578
May 1961   CD: RCA/BMG 09026 618792/
                                             09026 618272

Sweden   Roos, piano   LP: Bluebell BELL 109
1978-1979

Mens jeg venter

New York   Taubman, piano   LP: RCA LM 2578/LSC 2578
May 1961   CD: RCA/BMG 09026 618792/
                                             09026 618272

Stockholm   Parsons, piano   CD: Bluebell ABCD 009
September 1974   Previously issued by Bluebell
                                         on LP

Og jeg vil ha mig en hjaertenskjaer

New York   Taubman, piano   LP: RCA LM 2578/LSC 2578
May 1961   CD: RCA/BMG 09026 618792/
                                             09026 618272

Stockholm   Parsons, piano   CD: Bluebell ABCD 009
September 1974   Previously issued by Bluebell
                                         on LP

Vaaren

Vienna   VPO   LP: Decca LXT 6185/SXL 6185
April 1965   Bokstedt

As far as can be ascertained, most of Nilsson's performances of songs by Grieg are sung in Swedish

Gruber

Silent night, holy night

Stockholm August 1963	Leven, organ	45: Decca CEP 5517/SEC 5517
Stockholm February 1977	Bondeman, organ	LP: Swedish Society SLT 33256

Handel

Joy to the world

Stockholm   Bondeman, organ   LP: Swedish Society SLT 33256
February 1977

See the conquering hero

Stockholm   Bondeman, organ   LP: Swedish Society SLT 33256
February 1977   Sung in German

Hopkins

We Three Kings of Orient are

Stockholm   Bondeman, organ   LP: Swedish Society SLT 33256
February 1977

Liebermann

Penelope: Excerpt (Penelope's aria)

Stockholm April 1959	Stockholm Opera Orchestra Ehrling Sung in Swedish	CD: Bluebell ABCD 055

Lillijebjorn

Fjorton ar tror jag visst att jag var

New York October 1983	Unpublished video recording of Met centennial gala

Lindblad

En ung flickas morgonbetraktelse

Sweden 1978-1979	Roos, piano	LP: Bluebell BELL 114

Frederick Loewe

My Fair Lady: Excerpt (I could have danced all night)

Location uncertain 1960	Orchestral ensemble	LP: Decca MET 201-203/ SET 201-203 LP: Decca D247 D3 CD: Decca 421 0462 Part of the gala sequence included in Karajan's recording of Die Fledermaus
New York November 1967	Wustman, piano	CD: Melodram MEL 18027
Sweden 1978-1979	Roos, piano	LP: Bluebell BELL 109

Marchesi

La folletta

New York   Wustman, piano   CD: Melodram MEL 18027
November 1967

Melartin

Gib' mir dein Herz

New York   Wustman, piano   CD: Melodram MEL 18027
November 1967

Morgonsang

New York   Wustman, piano   CD: Melodram MEL 18027
November 1967

Tjugo är

Stockholm   Parsons, piano   CD: Bluebell ABCD 009
September 1974   Previously issued by Bluebell
                                         on LP

Sweden   Roos, piano   LP: Bluebell BELL 109/BELL 114
1978-1979

Mendelssohn

Hark the herald angels sing

Stockholm   Bondeman, organ   LP: Swedish Society SLT 33256
February 1977

Mozart

Don Giovanni

Vienna June 1959	Role of Donna Anna L.Price, Ratti, Valletti, Siepi, Corena, Van Mill Vienna Opera Chorus VPO Leinsdorf	LP: RCA RE 25028-25031/ SER 4528-4531 LP: Decca D10 D4 Excerpts CD: Decca 421 8752
Prague February and March 1967	Role of Donna Anna Arroyo, Grist, Schreier, Talvela, Fischer-Dieskau Prague National Chorus & Orchestra Böhm	LP: DG 2711 006/2740 108/2740 119 LP: DG 2740 205/2740 222 CD: DG 429 8702/435 3942 Excerpts LP: DG 2537 014/2538 098/2721 206

Don Giovanni:Excerpt (Or sai chi l'onore)

London May 1958	Philharmonia Wallberg	LP: Columbia 33CX 1629/SAX 2284 LP: Angel 35715/60353 LP: EMI 1C 187 00786-00787 CD: EMI CDM 763 1082

Nielsen

Aebleblornst

New York November 1967	Wustman, piano	CD: Hunt CDLSMH 34049 CD: Melodram MEL 18027
Sweden 1978-1979	Roos, piano	LP: Bluebell BELL 114

Den forste laerke

New York November 1967	Wustman, piano	CD: Hunt CDLSMH 34049 CD: Melodram MEL 18027

Nordqvist

Det var en gnaeng

Sweden   Roos, piano   LP: Bluebell BELL 114
1978-1979

Peterson-Berger

Aspakerspolska

Sweden   Roos, piano   LP: Bluebell BELL 109
1978-1979

Visa ei svensk volkston

Sweden   Roos, piano   LP: Bluebell BELL 114
1978-1979

Piccini

Alessandro nelle India: Excerpt (Se il ciel mi divide)

New York   Wustman, piano   CD: Hunt CDLSMH 34049
November 1967   CD: Melodram MEL 18027

Puccini

La fanciulla del West

Milan July 1958	Role of Minnie Carturan, Gibin, Ercolani, Sordello, Zaccaria La Scala Chorus and Orchestra Matacic	LP: Columbia 33CX 1631-1633/ SAX 2286-2288 LP: Angel 3593/SIC 6074 LP: EMI SLS 5079 CD: EMI CMS 763 9702

Gianni Schicchi: Excerpt (O mio babbino caro)

Sweden 1978-1979	Roos, piano	LP: Bluebell BELL 109/BELL 114

Tosca

Philadelphia April 1963	Role of Tosca Tagliavini, Vinay Philadelphia Opera Association Chorus & Orchestra Moresca	CD: Melodram CDM 270112
Rome June 1966	Role of Tosca Corelli, Fischer-Dieskau Santa Cecilia Chorus & Orchestra Maazel	LP: Decca MET 341-342/SET 341-342 CD: Decca 440 0512 <u>Vissi d'arte</u> CD: Decca 421 3152/421 3232
New York February 1969	Role of Tosca Domingo, Dooley Metropolitan Opera Chorus & Orchestra Schick	CD: Nuova Era NE 2286-2287 <u>Excerpts</u> CD: Memories HR 4275-4276

<u>Another recording of the opera may be preserved, as a Metropolitan opera broadcast with Nilsson in the title role took place in April 1963</u>

Tosca: Excerpt (Vissi d'arte)

Philadelphia January 1962	Philadelphia Orchestra Stokowski	LP: Melodram MEL 228
Stockholm January 1961	Stockholm RO Grevillius	CD: Bluebell ABCD 055
Moscow September 1964	Tonini, piano	LP: HRE Records HRE 340 CD: Legato LCD 147
New York November 1967	Wustman, piano	CD: Hunt CDLSMH 34049 CD: Melodram MEL 18027
Sweden 1978-1979	Roos, piano	LP: Bluebell BELL 109

Turandot

Milan December 1958	Role of Turandot Carteri, Di Stefano, Modesti La Scala Chorus and Orchestra Votto	LP: Cetra LO 84 Also issued on LP by Ed Smith
Rome 1960	Role of Turandot Tebaldi, Björling, Tozzi Rome Opera Chorus and Orchestra Leinsdorf	LP: RCA RE 25020-25022/LSC 6149 SER 4520-4522/SER 5643-5645 LP: RCA 26.35116 CD: RCA/BMG RD 85932
New York March 1961	Role of Turandot Moffo, Corelli, Giaiotti Metropolitan Opera Chorus & Orchestra Stokowski	LP: HRE Records HRE 299 CD: Metropolitan Opera MET 16 CD: Memories HR 4535-4536 Also issued on LP by Metropolitan Opera
Vienna June 1961	Role of Turandot L.Price, Di Stefano, Zaccaria Vienna Opera Chorus VPO Molinari-Pradelli	LP: Morgan MOR 6101 LP: HRE Records HRE 321
Milan July 1964	Role of Turandot Vishnevskaya, Corelli, Zaccaria La Scala Chorus and Orchestra Gavazzeni	LP: Edizione lirica EL 003 CD: Nuova Era 013.6318-6319 Excerpts CD: Memories HR 4275-4276
Rome 1965	Role of Turandot Scotto, Corelli, Giaiotti Rome Opera Chorus and Orchestra Molinari-Pradelli	LP: EMI AN 159-161/SAN 159-161 LP: Angel 3671 LP: EMI SLS 921/EX 29 02863 CD: EMI CMS 769 3272 Excerpts LP: EMI ASD 2403/ESD 100 3821 LP: EMI 1C 187 00786-00787
New York December 1966	Role of Turandot Freni, Corelli, Giaiotti Metropolitan Opera Chorus & Orchestra Mehta	LP: GOP Records GFC 17

Other recordings of the opera may be preserved, as Metropolitan opera broadcasts with Nilsson in the role of Turandot also took place in February 1962 and January 1965

Turandot: Excerpt (In questa reggia)

Stockholm August 1961	Stockholm RO Grevillius	CD: Bluebell ABCD 055
Moscow September 1964	La Scala Orchestra Gavazzeni	LP: HRE Records HRE 340 CD: Legato LCD 147
New York 1966	Bell Telephone Orchestra Voshees	LP: HRE Records HRE 379 CD: GOP Records GOP 736 <u>Broadcast in January 1967</u>

Turandot: Excerpts (Straniero ascolta; Principessa di morte)

Moscow September 1964	Prevedi, Gullino La Scala Chorus and Orchestra Gavazzeni	LP: HRE Records HRE 340 CD: Legato LCD 147

Rangstroem

Bön till natten

Vienna April 1965	VPO Bokstedt	LP: Decca LXT 6185/SXL 6185

En gammal dansrytm

Vienna April 1965	VPO Bokstedt	LP: Decca LXT 6185/SXL 6185

Flickan under nymänen

Stockholm September 1974	Parsons, piano	CD: Bluebell ABCD 009 Previously issued by Bluebell on LP
Sweden 1978-1979	Roos, piano	LP: Bluebell BELL 109

Melodi

Vienna April 1965	VPO Bokstedt	LP: Decca LXT 6185/SXL 6185

Sköldmön

Vienna April 1965	VPO Bokstedt	LP: Decca LXT 6185/SXL 6185
Stockholm September 1974	Parsons, piano	CD: Bluebell ABCD 009 Previously issued by Bluebell on LP

Runbaeck-Wikander

Frid

Stockholm February 1977	Bondeman, organ	LP: Swedish Society SLT 33256

Schubert

An die Musik

New York April 1961	Taubman, piano	LP: RCA LM 2578/LSC 2578

Auflösung

New York November 1967	Wustman, piano	CD: Hunt CDLSMH 34049 CD: Melodram MEL 18027 CD: Memories HR 4275-4276

Dem Unendlichen

New York April 1961	Taubman, piano	LP: RCA LM 2578/LSC 2578
New York November 1967	Wustman, piano	CD: Hunt CDLSMH 34049 CD: Melodram MEL 18027 CD: Memories HR 4275-4276

Die junge Nonne

New York November 1967	Wustman, piano	CD: Hunt CDLSMH 34049 CD: Melodram MEL 18027 CD: Memories HR 4275-4276

Nur wer die Sehnsucht kennt (Mignon)

New York April 1961	Taubman, piano	LP: RCA LM 2578/LSC 2578

Seligkeit

New York November 1967	Wustman, piano	CD: Hunt CDLSMH 34049 CD: Melodram MEL 18027

Sibelius

Demanten pa marssnoen

Vienna April 1965	VPO Bokstedt	LP: Decca LXT 6185/SXL 6185

Den förste kyssen

New York April 1961	Taubman, piano	LP: RCA LM 2578/LSC 2578
Stockholm September 1974	Parsons, piano	CD: Bluebell ABCD 009 Previously issued by Bluebell on LP
Sweden January 1975	Solyom, piano	LP: Bis BISLP 15 CD: Bis BISCD 15

Flickan kom ifran sin älsklings möte

Vienna April 1965	VPO Bokstedt	LP: Decca LXT 6185/SXL 6185
Sweden January 1975	Solyom, piano	LP: Bis BISLP 15 CD: Bis BISCD 15
Sweden 1978-1979	Roos, piano	LP: Bluebell BELL 109

Höstkväll

Vienna April 1965	VPO Bokstedt	LP: Decca LXT 6185/SXL 6185
New York November 1967	Wustman, piano	CD: Hunt CDLSMH 34049 CD: Melodram MEL 18027

Illalle

Sweden January 1975	Solyom, piano	LP: Bis BISLP 15 CD: Bis BISCD 15

Im Feld ein Mädchen singt

Sweden January 1975	Solyom, piano	LP: Bis BISLP 15 CD: Bis BISCD 15

Pa verandan vid hasvet

Sweden January 1975	Solyom, piano	LP: Bis BISLP 15 CD: Bis BISCD 15

Säv säv susa

New York April 1961	Taubman, piano	LP: RCA LM 2578/LSC 2578
Vienna April 1965	VPO Bokstedt	LP: Decca LXT 6185/SXL 6185
New York November 1967	Wustman, piano	CD: Hunt CDLSMH 34049 CD: Melodram MEL 18027
Sweden January 1975	Solyom, piano	LP: Bis BISLP 15 CD: Bis BISCD 15

Se'n har jag ej fragat mera

Sweden January 1975	Solyom, piano	LP: Bis BISLP 15 CD: Bis BISCD 15

Svarta rosor

New York April 1961	Taubman, piano	LP: RCA LM 2578/LSC 2578
Vienna April 1965	VPO Bokstedt	LP: Decca LXT 6185/SXL 6185
Sweden January 1975	Solyom, piano	LP: Bis BISLP 15 CD: Bis BISCD 15
Sweden 1978-1979	Roos, piano	LP: Bluebell BELL 109

Til kvällen

Stockholm September 1974	Parsons, piano	CD: Bluebell ABCD 009 Previously issued by Bluebell on LP

The tryst

New York April 1961	Taubman, piano	LP: RCA LM 2578/LSC 2578

Var det en dröm ?

New York April 1961	Taubman, piano	LP: RCA LM 2578/LSC 2578
Vienna April 1965	VPO Bokstedt	LP: Decca LXT 6185/SXL 6185
Stockholm September 1974	Parsons, piano	CD: Bluebell ABCD 009 Previously issued by Bluebell on LP
Sweden January 1975	Solyom, piano	LP: Bis BISLP 15 CD: Bis BISCD 15
Sweden 1978-1979	Roos, piano	LP: Bluebell BELL 114

Våren flyktar hastigt

Vienna April 1965	VPO Bokstedt	LP: Decca LXT 6185/SXL 6185
Stockholm September 1974	Parsons, piano	CD: Bluebell ABCD 009 Previously issued by Bluebell on LP
Sweden January 1975	Solyom, piano	LP: Bis BISLP 15 CD: Bis BISCD 15

32ème REPRÉSENTATION  VENDREDI 5 NOVEMBRE 1976
A 20 HEURES

ELEKTRA
VON RICHARD STRAUSS

TRAGÖDIE IN EINEM AUFZUGE VON HUGO VON HOFMANNSTHAL

DIRECTION MUSICALE **HORST STEIN**

MISE EN SCÈNE **AUGUST EVERDING**

DÉCOR ET COSTUMES **ANDRZEI MAJEWSKI**

DISTRIBUTION

KLYTAEMNESTRA	CHRISTA LUDWIG
ELEKTRA	BIRGIT NILSSON
CHRYSOTHEMIS	TERESA KUBIAK
AEGISTH	LOUIS RONEY
OREST	HANS SOTIN
DER PFLEGER DES OREST	JEAN-LOUIS SOUMAGNAS
DIE VERTRAUTE	MARTINE CLAVENCY
DIE SCHLEPPTRAEGERIN	MARYSE ACERRA
EIN JUNGER DIENER	ROBERT DUMÉ
EIN ALTER DIENER	JEAN RALLO
DIE AUFSEHERIN	HELIA T'HEZAN
FÜNF MÄGDE	JOCELYNE TAILLON
	HUGUETTE BRACHET
	ANNA RINGART
	HÉLÈNE GARETTI
	ÉLIANE LUBLIN

CHEF DES CHŒURS
JEAN LAFORGE

RESPONSABLE DU MAINTIEN DE LA MISE EN SCÈNE
MICHAEL DITTMANN

CHEFS DE CHANT
NADIA GEDDA-NOVA - THÉRÈSE COCHET

Elektra

Characters in order of appearance

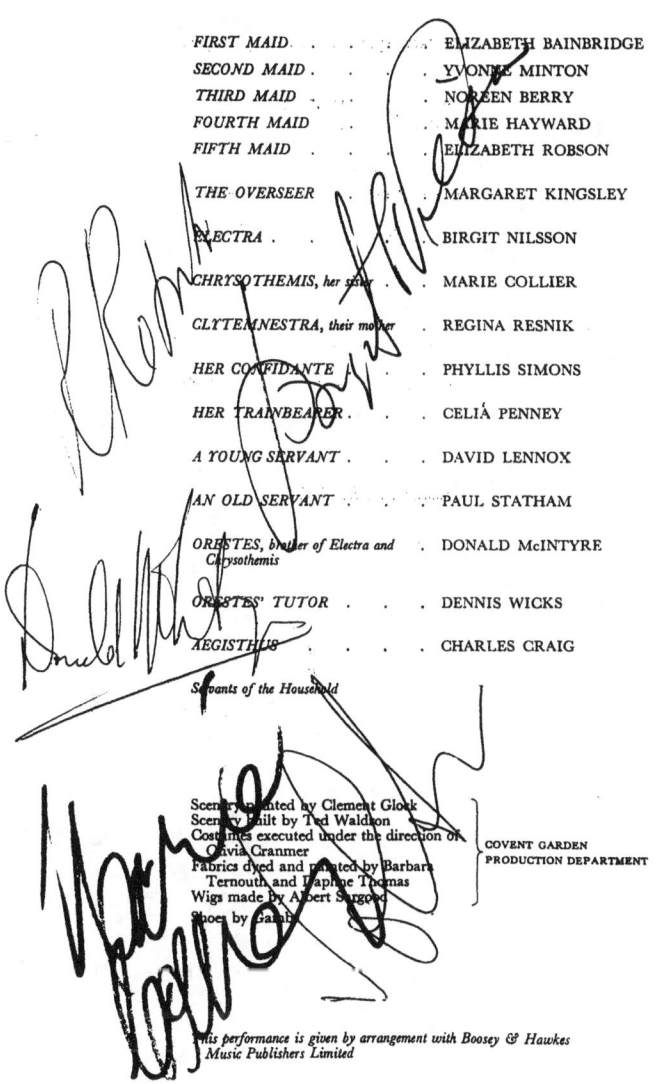

FIRST MAID	ELIZABETH BAINBRIDGE
SECOND MAID	YVONNE MINTON
THIRD MAID	NOREEN BERRY
FOURTH MAID	MARIE HAYWARD
FIFTH MAID	ELIZABETH ROBSON
THE OVERSEER	MARGARET KINGSLEY
ELECTRA	BIRGIT NILSSON
CHRYSOTHEMIS, her sister	MARIE COLLIER
CLYTEMNESTRA, their mother	REGINA RESNIK
HER CONFIDANTE	PHYLLIS SIMONS
HER TRAINBEARER	CELIA PENNEY
A YOUNG SERVANT	DAVID LENNOX
AN OLD SERVANT	PAUL STATHAM
ORESTES, brother of Electra and Chrysothemis	DONALD McINTYRE
ORESTES' TUTOR	DENNIS WICKS
AEGISTHUS	CHARLES CRAIG

Servants of the Household

Scenery painted by Clement Glock
Scenery built by Ted Waldron
Costumes executed under the direction of Olivia Cranmer
Fabrics dyed and painted by Barbara Ternouth and Daphne Thomas
Wigs made by Albert Sargood
Shoes by Gamba

COVENT GARDEN
PRODUCTION DEPARTMENT

This performance is given by arrangement with Boosey & Hawkes Music Publishers Limited

13 May 1969

Sieczynski

Wien, du Stadt meiner Träume

Stockholm September 1974	Parsons, piano	CD: Bluebell ABCD 009 Previously issued by Bluebell on LP
Sweden 1978-1979	Roos, piano	LP: Bluebell BELL 109

Sjoergen

Jeg giver digt til vaaren

Sweden   Roos, piano   LP: Bluebell BELL 109/BELL 114
1978-1979

Soederman

Den hvide roerde rosa

Sweden   Roos, piano   LP: Bluebell BELL 114
1978-1979

Stenhammer

Adagio

Sweden   Roos, piano   LP: Bluebell BELL 114
1978-1979

Flickan knyter e Johannesnatten; Flickan kom

New York   Wustman, piano   CD: Melodram MEL 18027
November 1967

I skogen

Sweden   Roos, piano   LP: Bluebell BELL 109
1978-1979

Richard Strauss

Elektra

Vienna December 1965	Role of Elektra Rysanek, Resnik, Windgassen, Wächter Vienna Opera Chorus VPO Böhm	LP: HRE Records HRE 314 CD: Legato SRO 833
Vienna June, September and November 1966 and February and June 1967	Role of Elektra Collier, Resnik, Stolze, Krause Vienna Opera Chorus VPO Solti	LP: Decca MET 354-355/ SET 354-355 CD: Decca 417 3452 Excerpts CD: Decca 421 3232
New York February 1980	Role of Elektra Rysanek, Dunn, Nagy, McIntyre Metropolitan Opera Chorus & Orchestra Levine	Unpublished video recording

Other performances may be preserved, as Metropolitan opera broadcasts with Nilsson in the role of Elektra took place in December 1966 and February 1971

Elektra: Excerpts (Ah! Das Gesicht!..Ich kann nicht sitzen; Closing scene)

Vienna September 1975	Rysanek VPO Böhm	LP: Legendary LR 101

Die Frau ohne Schatten

Munich September 1976	Role of Färberin Bjoner, Varnay, King, Kohn, Fischer-Dieskau Bavarian State Chorus & Orchestra Sawallisch	CD: Legendary LRCD 1029 Previously issued by Legendary on LP
Vienna October 1977	Role of Färberin Rysanek, Hesse, King, Berry, Wimberger Vienna Opera Chorus VPO Böhm	LP: HRE Records HRE 322 LP: DG 415 4721 CD: DG 415 4722

Salome

Vienna October 1961	Role of Salome G.Hoffman, Stolze, Kmennt, Wächter VPO Solti	LP: Decca MET 228-229/ SET 228-229 CD: Decca 414 4142 Closing scene LP: Decca LXT 6261/SXL 6261

Another performance may be preserved, as a Metropolitan opera broadcast with Nilsson in the role of Salome took place in March 1965

Salome: Excerpt (Closing scene)

Stockholm 1954	Bergstrom, Hendriksen Stockholm Opera Orchestra Ehrling Sung in Swedish	CD: Legato SRO 833 This excerpt begins at Es ist kein Laut zu vernehmen
New York April 1972	Metropolitan Opera Orchestra Böhm	LP: DG 2530 260/2721 206

Frühling (4 letzte Lieder)

Stockholm January 1970	Stockholm RO Segerstam	CD: Bluebell ABCD 009 Previously issued by Bluebell on LP

September (4 letzte Lieder)

Stockholm January 1970	Stockholm RO Segerstam	CD: Bluebell ABCD 009 Previously issued by Bluebell on LP

Beim Schlafengehen (4 letzte Lieder)

Stockholm January 1970	Stockholm RO Segerstam	CD: Bluebell ABCD 009 Previously issued by Bluebell on LP

Im Abendrot (4 letzte Lieder)

Stockholm January 1970	Stockholm RO Segerstam	CD: Bluebell ABCD 009 Previously issued by Bluebell on LP

Allerseelen

Sweden January 1975	Solyom, piano	LP: Bis BISLP 15 CD: Bis BISCD 15

Befreit

Sweden January 1975	Solyom, piano	LP: Bis BISLP 15 CD: Bis BISCD 15

Cäcilie

New York April 1961	Taubman, piano	LP: RCA LM 2578/LSC 2578
Sweden January 1975	Solyom, piano	LP: Bis BISLP 15 CD: Bis BISCD 15

Freundliche Vision

New York November 1967	Wustman, piano	CD: Hunt CDLSMH 34049 CD: Melodram MEL 10027 CD: Memories HR 4275-4276

Kornblumen

New York November 1967	Wustman, piano	CD: Hunt CDLSMH 34049 CD: Melodram MEL 18027 CD: Memories HR 4275-4276

Morgen

Stockholm
September 1974

Parsons, piano

CD: Bluebell ABCD 009
Previously issued by Bluebell
on LP

Die Nacht

Stockholm
September 1974

Parsons, piano

CD: Bluebell ABCD 009
Previously issued by Bluebell
on LP

Ruhe, meine Seele

Sweden
January 1975

Solyom, piano

LP: Bis BISLP 15
CD: Bis BISCD 15

Ständchen

Sweden
January 1975

Solyom, piano

LP: Bis BISLP 15
CD: Bis BISCD 15

Wiegenlied

New York
November 1967

Wustman, piano

CD: Hunt CDLSMH 34049
CD: Melodram MEL 18027
CD: Memories HR 4275-4276

Stockholm
September 1974

Parsons, piano

CD: Bluebell ABCD 009
Previously issued by Bluebell
on LP

Sweden
January 1975

Solyom, piano

LP: Bis BISLP 15
CD: Bis BISCD 15

Zueignung

New York
November 1967

Wustman, piano

CD: Hunt CDLSMH 34049
CD: Melodram MEL 18027
CD: Memories HR 4275-4276

Stockholm
September 1974

Parsons, piano

CD: Bluebell ABCD 009
Previously issued by Bluebell
on LP

Sweden
January 1975

Solyom, piano

LP: Bis BISLP 15
CD: Bis BISCD 15

Verdi

Aida

Rome	Role of Aida	LP: EMI AN 189-191/SAN 189-191
June and	Bumbry, Corelli,	LP: Angel 3716
July 1965	Sereni	LP: EMI SLS 929
	Rome Opera	CD: EMI CMS 763 2292
	Chorus & Orchestra	Excerpts
	Mehta	LP: EMI ASD 2543
		LP: EMI 1C 187 00786-00787
		CD: EMI CDM 764 0352/CD-EMX 2174

Another performance of the opera may be preserved, as a Metropolitan opera broadcast with Nilsson in the role of Aida took place in March 1965

Aida: Excerpt (Ritorna vincitor)

London	Philharmonia	45: Columbia SEL 1584
May 1957	L.Ludwig	LP: Columbia 33CX 1522
		LP: Angel 35540
		LP: EMI 1C 187 00786-00787
Walthamstow	Covent Garden	LP: Decca LXT 6068/SXL 6068
April 1963	Orchestra	LP: Decca 411 8851
	Pritchard	

Aida: Excerpt (Fu la sorte dell' armi)

Walthamstow	G.Hoffman	LP: Decca LXT 6068/SXL 6068
April 1963	Covent Garden	
	Orchestra	
	Pritchard	

Aida: Excerpt (O patria mia)

London May 1957	Philharmonia L.Ludwig	45: Columbia SEL 1584 LP: Columbia 33CX 1522 LP: Angel 35540 LP: EMI 1C 187 00786-00787
Stockholm August 1961	Stockholm PO Grevillius	CD: Bluebell ABCD 055
Walthamstow April 1963	Covent Garden Orchestra Pritchard	LP: Decca LXT 6068/SXL 6068

Aida: Excerpt (O ciel! Mio padre!)

Philadelphia January 1962	G.London Philadelphia Orchestra Stokowski	LP: Melodram MEL 228
Walthamstow April 1963	Ottolini, L.Quilico Covent Garden Orchestra Pritchard	LP: Decca LXT 6068/SXL 6068

Aida: Excerpt (La fatal pietra....O terra addio)

Walthamstow April 1963	Ottolini Covent Garden Orchestra Pritchard	LP: Decca LXT 6068/SXL 6068

Un Ballo in maschera

Rome July 1960 and July 1961	Role of Amelia Stahlman, Simionato, Bergonzi, MacNeil, Krause Santa Cecilia Chorus & Orchestra Solti	LP: Decca MET 215-217/SET 215-217 CD: Decca 425 6552 Excerpts LP: Decca LXT 6013/SXL 6013 LP: Decca 414 8851 CD: Decca 421 3232
New York January 1963	Role of Amelia Dobbs, Madeira, Tucker, Merrill, Reitan Metropolitan Opera Chorus & Orchestra Santi	LP: Hope Records HOPE 236

Un Ballo in maschera: Excerpt (Ecco l'orrido campo)

Munich Date uncertain	Bavarian RO Erede	LP: Melodram MEL 653
London May 1957	Philharmonia L.Ludwig	45: Columbia SEL 1606 LP: Columbia 33CX 1522 LP: Angel 35540 LP: EMI 1C 187 00786-00787

Don Carlo: Excerpt (O don fatale)

Walthamstow April 1962	Covent Garden Orchestra Quadri	LP: Decca LXT 6033/SXL 6033

La Forza del destino: Excerpt (Madre, pietosa vergine)

Walthamstow April 1962	Covent Garden Orchestra Quadri	LP: Decca LXT 6033/SXL 6033 LP: Decca 411 8851

La Forza del destino: Excerpt (Pace, pace, mio Dio!)

London May 1957	Philharmonia L.Ludwig	45: Columbia SEL 1606 LP: Columbia 33CX 1522 LP: Angel 35540
Stockholm January 1961	Stockholm RO Grevillius	CD: Bluebell ABCD 055
Walthamstow April 1962	Covent Garden Orchestra Quadri	LP: Decca LXT 6033/SXL 6033

Saturday, 8th October, 1960

The 88th performance at the Royal Opera House

of

Götterdämmerung

MUSIC DRAMA IN A PROLOGUE AND THREE ACTS

(being the third day of the Trilogy
" Der Ring des Nibelungen ")

Words and music by Richard Wagner

Scenery and costumes by Leslie Hurry

CONDUCTOR — RUDOLF KEMPE

Production rehearsed by Erich Witte

THE COVENT GARDEN ORCHESTRA
Leader — Charles Taylor

THE COVENT GARDEN OPERA CHORUS
Chorus Master — Douglas Robinson

This opera was first produced at the Festspielhaus, Bayreuth, 17th August, 1876, with Georg Unger, Eugen Gura, Gustav Siehr, Karl Hill, Amalie Materna, Mathilde Weckerlin, Luise Jaide, Johanna Wagner, Josephine Schefsky, Friedericke Sadler Grün, Lilli Lehmann, Marie Lehmann, Minna Lammert, conductor Hans Richter. It was first performed in London at Her Majesty's Theatre, 9th May, 1882, conductor Seidl; at Covent Garden, 13th July, 1892, with Max Alvary, Julius Knapp, Wiegand, Lissmann, Katherina Klafsky, Senger-Bettaque, Schumann-Heink, conductor Mahler.

CHARACTERS IN ORDER OF APPEARANCE

FIRST NORN	MARJORIE THOMAS
SECOND NORN	MONICA SINCLAIR
THIRD NORN	UNA HALE
BRÜNNHILDE	BIRGIT NILSSON
SIEGFRIED	WOLFGANG WINDGASSEN
GUNTHER	HERMANN UHDE
HAGEN	GOTTLOB FRICK
GUTRUNE	AMY SHUARD
WALTRAUTE	URSULA BÖSE
ALBERICH	OTAKAR KRAUS
WOGLINDE	JOAN CARLYLE
WELLGUNDE	JOSEPHINE VEASEY
FLOSSHILDE	MARJORIE THOMAS

DER RING DES NIBELUNGEN

A stage-festival play for three days and a preliminary evening (Ein Bühnenfestspiel für drei Tage und einen Vorabend), words and music by Richard Wagner.

The first performance of the entire Cycle took place at the Festspielhaus, Bayreuth on 13th, 14th, 16th and 17th August, 1876. Das Rheingold had been given on 22nd September, 1869, at the Royal Court Theatre, Munich, and Die Walküre at the same theatre on 26th June, 1870.

The first complete Cycle in London was given at Her Majesty's Theatre on 5th, 6th, 8th and 9th May, 1882, under Anton Seidl and sung in German.

The first Cycle at Covent Garden took place in June, 1892, but the four operas were given in this order: Siegfried, Rheingold, Walküre, Götterdämmerung, so that the tenor, Max Alvary, could make his Covent Garden debut as the young Siegfried. This first complete RING in English was sung at Covent Garden under Hans Richter in January, 1908.

BAYREUTHER FESTSPIELE
MITTWOCH, 1. AUGUST 1962

RICHARD WAGNER
DER RING DES NIBELUNGEN · EIN BÜHNENFESTSPIEL FÜR DREI TAGE UND EINEN VORABEND
DRITTER TAG: GÖTTERDÄMMERUNG

SIEGFRIED	HANS HOPF	
GUNTHER	MARCEL CORDES	
HAGEN	GOTTLOB FRICK	
ALBERICH	OTAKAR KRAUS	
BRÜNNHILDE	BIRGIT NILSSON	
GUTRUNE	JUTTA MEYFARTH	
WALTRAUTE	MARGARETE BENCE	
1. NORN	ELISABETH SCHÄRTEL	
2. NORN	GRACE HOFFMAN	
3. NORN	GERTRAUD HOPF	
WOGLINDE	GUNDULA JANOWITZ	
WELLGUNDE	ELISABETH SCHWARZENBERG	
FLOSSHILDE	SIEGLINDE WAGNER	

MUSIKALISCHE LEITUNG	RUDOLF KEMPE
REGIE UND INSZENIERUNG	WOLFGANG WAGNER
CHOREINSTUDIERUNG	WILHELM PITZ
MUSIKALISCHE ASSISTENZ	PAUL ZELTER · WALTER BORN
REGIE-ASSISTENZ	ALFRED WALTER
	MANFRED LINKE
KOSTÜM	KURT PALM
MASKE	WILLI KLOSE
AUSSTATTUNGSLEITUNG	
PROJEKTIONEN	HANS-WOLFGANG DAHM
TECHNISCHE LEITUNG	REINHARD KRUMM
BELEUCHTUNG	JAKOB SCHLOSSTEIN

DER BEGINN JEDES AUFZUGES WIRD 15 MINUTEN VORHER MIT EINER FANFARE, 10 MINUTEN VORHER MIT ZWEI UND 5 MINUTEN VORHER MIT DREI FANFAREN ANGEKÜNDIGT

BEGINN: 16.00 UHR · II. AUFZUG 19.15 UHR · III. AUFZUG 21.30 UHR · ENDE GEGEN 22.50 UHR · NACH BEGINN DER AUFZÜGE KEIN EINLASS

Macbeth

Rome July 1964	Role of Lady Macbeth Prevedi, Taddei, Foiani Santa Cecilia Chorus & Orchestra Schippers	LP: Decca MET 282-284/ SET 282-284 CD: Decca 433 0392

Macbeth: Excerpt (Vieni t'affretta/Or tutti sorgete)

Walthamstow April 1962	Covent Garden Orchestra Quadri	45: Decca CEP 5525/SEC 5525 LP: Decca LXT 6033/SXL 6033 LP: Decca 411 8851 CD: Decca 421 3232
Moscow September 1964	Tonini, piano	LP: HRE Records HRE 340 CD: Legato LCD 147
New York 1966	Bell Telephone Orchestra Voshees	LP: HRE Records HRE 379

Macbeth: Excerpt (La luce langue)

Walthamstow April 1962	Covent Garden Orchestra Quadri	LP: Decca LXT 6033/SXL 6033 LP: Decca 411 8851 CD: Decca 421 3232

Macbeth: Excerpt (Una macchia è qui tutt' ora)

Walthamstow April 1962	Covent Garden Orchestra Quadri	45: Decca CEP 5525/SEC 5525 LP: Decca LXT 6033/SXL 6033 LP: Decca 411 8851 CD: Decca 421 3232

Nabucco: Excerpt (Ben io t'invenni/Anch'io dischiuso/Salgo già)

Walthamstow April 1962	Covent Garden Orchestra Quadri	LP: Decca LXT 6033/SXL 6033 LP: Decca 411 8851

Requiem

Boston 1965	Soprano soloist Chookasian, Bergonzi, Flagello Pro Musica Chorus Boston SO Leinsdorf	LP: RCA LSC 7040 LP: RCA RE 5537-8/SER 5537-8

Wagner

<u>Die Feen: Excerpt (Weh mir! So nah die fürchterliche Stunde/Ich häufe selbst die Schrecken an)</u>

London 1972	LSO C.Davis	LP: Philips 6500 294

<u>Der fliegende Holländer: Excerpt (Traft ihr das Schiff im Meere an)</u>

London May 1957	Chorus Philharmonia L.Ludwig	LP: Columbia 33CX 1522 LP: Angel 35540 LP: EMI 1C 187 00786-00787 CD: EMI CDM 763 1082
London 1972	Alldis Choir LSO C.Davis	LP: Philips 6500 294

<u>Der fliegende Holländer: Excerpt (Wie aus der Ferne/Willst du des Vaters Wahl nicht schelten?)</u>

London May 1957	Hotter Philharmonia L.Ludwig	LP: Columbia 33CX 1542/SAX 2296 LP: Regal SREG 2068 LP: EMI SXLP 30557 CD: EMI CMS 764 0082

Götterdämmerung

Munich September 1955	Role of Brünnhilde Rysanek, Malaniuk, Aldenhoff, Uhde, Frick Bavarian State Chorus & Orchestra Knappertsbusch	LP: Melodram MEL 425
Bayreuth August 1960	Role of Brünnhilde Bjoner, G.Hoffman, Hopf, Stewart, Frick, O.Kraus Bayreuth Festival Chorus & Orchestra Kempe	LP: Melodram MEL 609
Vienna May, June, October and November 1964	Role of Brünnhilde Watson, C.Ludwig, Windgassen, Frick, Fischer-Dieskau, Neidlinger Vienna Opera Chorus VPO Solti	LP: Decca MET 292-297/SET 292-297 LP: Decca D100 D19/RING 1-22 LP: Decca 414 1001/414 1151 CD: Decca 414 1002/414 1152 Excerpts LP: Decca LXT 6220/SXL 6220 LP: Decca LXT 6261/SXL 6261 LP: Decca GRV 24/417 1811 CD: Decca 421 3132
Bayreuth July and August 1967	Role of Brünnhilde Dvorakova, Mödl, Windgassen, Stewart, Greindl Bayreuth Festival Chorus & Orchestra Böhm	LP: Philips 6747 037/6747 049 CD: Philips 412 4882/420 3252 Excerpts LP: Philips 6575 503/6575 504 LP: Philips 6833 083

Other performances may be preserved, as Metropolitan opera broadcasts with Nilsson in the role of Brünnhilde took place in January 1962, December 1963 and March 1975

Götterdämmerung: Excerpt (Starke Scheite schichtet mir dort)

Philadelphia January 1962	Philadelphia Orchestra Stokowski	LP: Melodram MEL 228

Lohengrin

Bayreuth August 1954	Role of Elsa Varnay, Windgassen, Adam, Uhde, Fischer-Dieskau Bayreuth Festival Chorus & Orchestra Jochum	LP: Cetra LO 77 LP: Melodram MEL 541 CD: Laudis LCD 44015 CD: Melodram MEL 36104 Excerpts LP: Gioielli della lirica GML 20 CD: Memories HR 4275-4276

Lohengrin: Excerpt (Einsam in trüben Tagen)

London May 1957	Philharmonia L.Ludwig	LP: Columbia 33CX 1522 LP: Angel 35540 LP: EMI 1C 187 00786-00787 CD: EMI CDM 763 1082
London June 1963	Covent Garden Downes	LP: Decca LXT 6077/SXL 6077 LP: Decca GRV 24

Parsifal: Excerpt (Dies alles hab' ich nun geträumt/Ich sah das Kind....... to end Act 2)

London 1974	Brilioth, Bailey Covent Garden Orchestra Segerstam	LP: Philips 6500 661

Rienzi: Excerpt (Gerechter Gott!)

London 1972	LSO C.Davis	LP: Philips 6500 294

Thursday, 6th October, 1960

The 112th performance at the Royal Opera House

of

Siegfried

MUSIC DRAMA IN THREE ACTS

(being the second day of the Trilogy "Der Ring des Nibelungen")

Words and music by Richard Wagner

Scenery and costumes by Leslie Hurry

CONDUCTOR — RUDOLF KEMPE

Production rehearsed by Erich Witte

THE COVENT GARDEN ORCHESTRA
Leader — Charles Taylor

This opera was first produced at the Festspielhaus, Bayreuth on 16th August, 1876, with Georg Unger, Karl Schlosser, Franz Betz, Karl Hill, Franz von Reichenberg, Amalie Materna, Luisa Jaide, Marie Haupt, conductor Hans Richter. It was first performed in England at Her Majesty's Theatre, 8th May, 1882, conductor Seidl; at Covent Garden, 8th June, 1892, with Alvary, Lieban, Grengg, Wiegand, Lorent, Rosa, Sucher, Traubmann, Schumann-Heink, conductor Mahler.

CHARACTERS IN ORDER OF APPEARANCE

MIME	GERHARD STOLZE
SIEGFRIED	WOLFGANG WINDGASSEN
THE WANDERER, WOTAN	HANS HOTTER
ALBERICH	OTAKAR KRAUS
FAFNER, the Dragon	MICHAEL LANGDON
THE WOODBIRD	JOAN CARLYLE
ERDA	MARGA HÖFFGEN
BRÜNNHILDE	BIRGIT NILSSON

DER RING DES NIBELUNGEN

A stage-festival play for three days and a preliminary evening (Ein Bühnenfestspiel für drei Tage und einem Vorabend) words and music by Richard Wagner.

The first performance of the entire Cycle took place at the Festspielhaus, Bayreuth on 13th, 14th, 16th and 17th August, 1876. Das Rheingold had been given on 22nd September, 1869, and Die Walküre at the same theatre on 26th June, 1870.

The first complete Cycle in London was given at Her Majesty's Theatre on 5th, 7th, 8th and 9th May, 1882, under Anton Seidl and sung in German.

The first Cycle at Covent Garden took place in June, 1892, but the four operas were given in this order: Siegfried, Rheingold, Walküre, Götterdämmerung, so that the tenor, Max Alvary, could make his Covent Garden debut as the young Siegfried. This first complete RING in English was sung at Covent Garden under Hans Richter in January, 1908.

LSO INTERNATIONAL SERIES

52nd Annual Series of Concerts presented by the London Symphony Orchestra Limited (Founded 1904) in association with the Arts Council of Great Britain the Greater London Council and the Peter Stuyvesant Foundation

London Symphony Orchestra
Leader John Georgiadis

Georg Solti
Conductor

Birgit Nilsson
Soloist

Beethoven

Symphony No. 4 in B flat

Scena, 'Abscheulicher', ('Fidelio')

Interval
A warning gong will be sounded for five minutes before the end of the interval

Strauss

Don Juan, Op. 20

Dance of the Seven Veils and Closing Scene ('Salome')

Tuesday 31 May at 8 pm at the Royal Festival Hall
General Manager John Denison CBE

Siegfried

Bayreuth July 1960	Role of Brünnhilde Siebert, Höffgen, Hopf, H.Kraus, Uhde, O.Kraus, Roth-Ehrang Bayreuth Festival Orchestra Kempe	LP: Melodram MEL 608
Vienna May, October and November 1962	Role of Brünnhilde Sutherland, Höffgen, Windgassen, Stolze, Hotter, Böhme, Neidlinger VPO Solti	LP: Decca MET 242-246/SET 242-246 LP: Decca D100 D19/RING 1-22 LP: Decca 414 1001/414 1101 CD: Decca 414 1002/414 1102 Excerpts LP: Decca LXT 6142/SXL 6142
Bayreuth July 1966	Role of Brünnhilde Köth, Soukupova, Windgassen, Wohlfahrt, Adam, Böhme, Neidlinger Bayreuth Festival Orchestra Böhm	LP: Philips 6747 037/6747 048 CD: Philips 412 4832/420 3252

Tannhäuser

Naples March 1956	Role of Venus Rysanek, Lustig, Terkal, Cordes, Frick San Carlo Opera Chorus & Orchestra Böhm	CD: Melodram MEL 37073
Berlin 1968	Roles of Elisabeth and Venus Windgassen, Laubenthal, Adam, Fischer-Dieskau Deutsche Oper Chorus & Orchestra Gerdes	LP: DG SLPM 139 284-139 287 LP: DG 2711 008/2740 142 Excerpts LP: DG 2721 206/2537 016/2638 098

Another performance may be preserved, as a Metropolitan opera broadcast with Nilsson in the roles of Elisabeth and Venus took place in March 1966

Tannhäuser: Excerpt (Dich teure Halle)

London May 1957	Philharmonia L.Ludwig	LP: Columbia 33CX 1522 LP: Angel 35540 LP: EMI 1C 187 00786-00787 CD: EMI CDM 763 1082
Stockholm March 1959	Stockholm PO Grevillius	CD: Bluebell ABCD 055
Stockholm 1959	Stockholm Opera Orchestra Ehrling	LP: HMV (Sweden) ALPC 1
London June 1963	Covent Garden Orchestra Downes	LP: Decca LXT 6077/SXL 6077 LP: Decca GRV 24
New York 1966	Bell Telephone Orchestra Voshees	LP: HRE Records HRE 379 CD: GOP Records GOP 736 Broadcast in January 1967

Tristan und Isolde

Florence May 1957	Role of Isolde G.Hoffman, Windgassen, Neidlinger, Rohr Maggio Musicale Chorus & Orchestra Rodzinski	LP: Cetra DOC 20
Bayreuth July 1957	Role of Isolde G.Hoffman, Windgassen, Hotter, Van Mill Bayreuth Festival Chorus & Orchestra Sawallisch	LP: Melodram MEL 575
Vienna September 1960	Role of Isolde Resnik, Uhl, Krause, Van Mill Vienna Opera Chorus VPO Solti	LP: Decca MET 204-208/SET 204-208 LP: Decca D41 D5 CD: Decca 430 2342 Excerpts LP: Decca LXT 6178/SXL 6178 CD: Decca 421 3232/421 8772 CD: Decca 440 0692 Original LP issue contained a bonus LP of rehearsal extracts
Bayreuth July 1962	Role of Isolde Meyer, Windgassen, Wächter, Greindl Bayreuth Festival Chorus & Orchestra Böhm	LP: Melodram MEL 625
Bayreuth July and August 1966	Role of Isolde C.Ludwig, Windgassen, Wächter, Talvela Bayreuth Festival Chorus & Orchestra Böhm	LP: DG KL 512-516/SKL 912-916 LP: DG LPM 139 221-139 225/ SLPM 139 221-139 225 LP: DG 2713 001/2740 144/415 3951 LP: Philips 6747 243 CD: DG 419 8892 CD: Philips 434 4202/434 4252 Excerpts LP: DG SLPEM 136 433/135 118 LP: DG 2705 015/2721 112/2721 115 LP: DG 2721 206/2535 243/2536 037 LP: DG 2537 001/2538 098/2538 245 LP: DG 410 8551 LP: Philips 6833 195 Original LP issue continued rehearsal extracts not involving Nilsson, but Philips LP 6701 048 did contain Liebesnacht rehearsal

Tristan und Isolde/continued

Bayreuth August 1966	Role of Isolde C.Ludwig, Windgassen, Wächter, Talvela Bayreuth Festival Chorus & Orchestra Böhm	CD: Frequenz CML 3 Excerpts CD: Curcio-Hunt OPV 16 CD: Memories HR 4275-4276 CD: Memories HR 4424-4425
Orange July 1973	Role of Isolde Hesse, Vickers, Berry, Rundgren New Philharmonia Chorus Orchestre National Böhm	LP: HRE Records HRE 359 CD: Rodolphe RPC 32553-32555
New York January 1974	Role of Isolde Wilma, Vickers, Dooley, Plishka Metropolitan Opera Chorus & Orchestra Leinsdorf	LP: ERR Records ERR 141 Source of this recording is not a Metropolitan opera broadcast

Other performances may be preserved, as Metropolitan opera broadcasts with Nilsson in the role of Isolde also took place in March 1961, February 1963 and and December 1971

Tristan und Isolde: Excerpt (Weh, ach wehe, dies zu dulden....der Trank ist's, der mir taugt)

Vienna September 1959	G.Hoffman VPO Knappertsbusch	LP: Decca LXT 5559/SXL 2184 LP: Decca JB 58
New York October 1983	Metropolitan Opera Orchestra Levine	Unpublished video recording of Metropolitan centennial gala Beginning only at Wie lachend sie mir Lieder singen

Tristan und Isolde: Excerpt (Tristan! Geliebter!....Liebesnacht)

Milan April 1959	Rössel-Majdan, Windgassen La Scala Orchestra Karajan	CD: Hunt CDKAR 224 Beginning only at Sink hernieder, Nacht der Liebe
New York January 1960	Dalis, Vinay Metropolitan Opera Orchestra Böhm	CD: Melodram CDM 26519
New York April 1981	Dunn, Vickers Metropolitan Opera Orchestra Levine	Unpublished radio broadcast Beginning only at Sink hernieder, Nacht der Liebe

Tuesday, 17th June, 1958

The 178th performance at the Royal Opera House
of

TRISTAN UND ISOLDE

OPERA IN THREE ACTS

Words and Music by RICHARD WAGNER
Sets and Costumes by LESLIE HURRY

CONDUCTOR — RAFAEL KUBELIK
PRODUCER — CHRISTOPHER WEST

THE COVENT GARDEN OPERA CHORUS
Chorus Master - DOUGLAS ROBINSON

THE COVENT GARDEN ORCHESTRA
Leader - CHARLES TAYLOR

CHARACTERS IN ORDER OF APPEARANCE

YOUNG SEAMAN	DERMOT TROY
ISOLDE	BIRGIT NILSSON
BRANGÄNE	IRENE DALIS
KURWENAL	OTAKAR KRAUS
TRISTAN	RAMON VINAY
MELOT	EDGAR EVANS
KING MARK	JAMES PEASE
SHEPHERD	DAVID TREE
STEERSMAN	RHYDDERCH DAVIES

RICHARD WAGNER, 1813 - 1883

This opera was first produced at the Court Theatre, Munich, on 10th June 1865, with Malvina Schnorr von Carolsfeld, Anna Deinet, Ludwig Schnorr von Carolsfeld, Zottmayer, and Anton Mitterwurzer; conductor Hans von Bülow. Its first performance in London was at Drury Lane on 20th June 1882 with Rosa Sucher, Marianne Brandt, Hermann Winkelmann, Ernst Kraus, Eugen Gura; conductor Hans Richter. It was first given at Covent Garden on 15th June 1892 with Rosa Sucher, Ernestine Schumann-Heink, Max Alvary, Herr Knapp and Heinrich Wiegand. Covent Garden Tristans have included Jean de Reszke, Jacques Urlus, Lauritz Melchior, Walter Widdop and Set Svanholm; while interpreters of Isolde in this theatre have included Lillian Nordica, Lilli Lehmann, Anna von Mildenburg, Felia Litvinne, Gertrud Kappel, Frida Leider, Kirsten Flagstad, Germaine Lubin, Astrid Varnay and Sylvia Fisher.

BAYREUTHER FESTSPIELE
MITTWOCH, 12. AUGUST 1964
RICHARD WAGNER
TRISTAN UND ISOLDE

MUSIKALISCHE LEITUNG · KARL BÖHM
REGIE UND INSZENIERUNG · WIELAND WAGNER
CHOREINSTUDIERUNG · WILHELM PITZ

TRISTAN · WOLFGANG WINDGASSEN
ISOLDE · BIRGIT NILSSON
KÖNIG MARKE · HANS HOTTER
KURWENAL · GUSTAV NEIDLINGER
BRANGÄNE · KERSTIN MEYER
MELOT · NIELS MÖLLER
HIRT · ERWIN WOHLFAHRT
SEEMANN · HERMANN WINKLER
STEUERMANN · HANNS HANNO DAUM

MASKE · WILLI KLOSE — BELEUCHTUNG
PAUL EBERHARDT / ERICH HAGER — BÜHNEN-
TECHNIK · REINHARD KRUMM — REGIEASSI-
STENZ · PETER LEHMANN — MUSIKALISCHE
ASSISTENZ · ALFRED WALTER / CLAUS ROESSNER

DER BEGINN JEDES AKTES WIRD 15 MINU-
TEN VORHER MIT EINER FANFARE, 10 MINU-
TEN VORHER MIT ZWEI UND 5 MINUTEN
VORHER MIT DREI FANFAREN ANGEKÜNDIGT.
1. AKT 16.00 UHR · 2. AKT 18.20 UHR · 3. AKT
20.40 UHR · ENDE GEGEN 21.50 UHR / NACH
BEGINN DER AKTE KEIN EINLASS

Tristan und Isolde: Excerpt (Mild und leise)

London May 1957	Philharmonia L.Ludwig	LP: Columbia 33CX 1522 LP: Angel 35540 LP: Columbia (Germany) SHZE 154 LP: EMI 1C 187 00786-00787 CD: EMI CDM 763 1082
Vienna September 1959	VPO Knappertsbusch	LP: Decca LXT 5559/SXL 2184 LP: Decca JB 58/GRV 24 CD: Decca 414 6252/433 3332/433 3402
Vienna May 1962	VPO Knappertsbusch	Unpublished video recording

Die Walküre

Bayreuth July 1954	Role of Ortlinde Varnay, Mödl, Milinkovic, Lorenz, Hotter, Greindl Bayreuth Festival Orchestra Keilberth	LP: Melodram MEL 547 CD: Melodram MEL 36102
Bayreuth August 1957	Role of Sieglinde Varnay, Milinkovic, Vinay, Hotter, Greindl Bayreuth Festival Orchestra Knappertsbusch	LP: Estro Armonico EA 032 LP: Discocorp IGI 292 LP: Cetra LO 59/DOC 48 LP: Melodram MEL 577 CD: Music and Arts CD 254 CD: Laudis LCD 44011/154 021
Walthamstow September 1961	Role of Brünnhilde Brouwenstijn, Gorr, Vickers, G.London, Ward LSO Leinsdorf	LP: RCA LD 6706/LDS 6706 LP: Decca 7BB 125-129 CD: Decca 430 3912 Excerpts LP: RCA RB 6658/SB 6658 LP: Decca SDD 430/GRV 24
Vienna October and November 1965	Role of Brünnhilde Crespin, C.Ludwig, King, Hotter, Frick VPO Solti	LP: Decca MET 312-316/SET 312-316 LP: Decca D100 D19/RING 1-22 LP: Decca 414 1001/414 1051 CD: Decca 414 1002/414 1052 Excerpts LP: Decca SET 390 CD: Decca 421 8872
Bayreuth July and August 1967	Role of Brünnhilde Rysanek, Burmeister, King, Adam, Nienstedt Bayreuth Festival Orchestra Böhm	LP: Philips 6747 037/6747 047 CD: Philips 412 4782/420 3252 Excerpts LP: Philips 6575 501/6575 504 LP: Philips 6833 083
New York March 1969	Role of Brünnhilde Crespin, Veasey, Vickers, Adam, Talvela Metropolitan Opera Orchestra Karajan	CD: Nuova Era NE 2405-2408 CD: Hunt CDKAR 217 Excerpts CD: Memories HR 4275-4276

Other performances may be preserved, as Metropolitan opera broadcasts with Nilsson in the role of Brünnhilde also took place in December 1961, February 1965, February 1968, December 1972 and March 1975

Die Walküre, Act 1

Hamburg Date uncertain	Role of Sieglinde Svanholm, Greindl NDR Orchestra Schmidt-Isserstedt	LP: HRE Records HRE 347

Die Walküre: Excerpt (Der Männer Sippe)

Hamburg 1953	NDR Orchestra Sandberg	LP: Melodram MEL 653
London June 1963	Covent Garden Orchestra Downes	LP: Decca LXT 6077/SXL 6077 LP: Decca GRV 24

Die Walküre: Excerpt (Du bist der Lenz)

Hamburg 1953	NDR Orchestra Sandberg	LP: Melodram MEL 653
London June 1963	Covent Garden Orchestra Downes	LP: Decca LXT 6077/SXL 6077 LP: Decca GRV 24

Die Walküre: Excerpt (Schläfst du, Gast?...to end Act 1)

London 1974	Brilioth Covent Garden Orchestra Segerstam	LP: Philips 6500 661
New York February 1975	Vickers Metropolitan Opera Orchestra Ehrling	LP: ERR Records ERR 141 <u>Source of this recording is not</u> <u>a Metropolitan opera broadcast</u>

Die Walküre: Excerpt (War es so schmählich?.....trotzt' ich deinem Gebot)

Hamburg 1953	S.Björling NDR Orchestra Sandberg	LP: Melodram MEL 653

Die Walküre: Excerpt (War es so schmählich?...to end of opera)

London May 1957	Hotter Philharmonia L.Ludwig	LP: Columbia 33CX 1542/SAX 2296 LP: Regal SREG 2068 LP: EMI SXLP 30557 CD: EMI CMS 565 2122

Die Walküre: Excerpt (Siegmund, sieh' auf mich)

Milan April 1958	Suthaus La Scala Orchestra Karajan	CD: Hunt CDKAR 223

Die Walküre: Excerpts (Kehrte der Vater nun heim; Schützt mich in höchster Not; Nicht sehre die Sorge um mich; Fort denn eile)

Bayreuth August 1965	Rysanek, King, Adam, Talvela Bayreuth Festival Orchestra Böhm	CD: Legato SRO 833

Der Engel (Wesendonk-Lieder)

New York April 1961	Taubman, piano	LP: RCA LM 2578/LSC 2578
London 1972	LSO C.Davis	LP: Philips 6500 294

Stehe still (Wesendonk-Lieder)

London 1972	LSO C.Davis	LP: Philips 6500 294

Im Treibhaus (Wesendonk-Lieder)

London 1972	LSO C.Davis	LP: Philips 6500 294

Schmerzen (Wesendonk-Lieder)

London 1972	LSO C.Davis	LP: Philips 6500 294

Träume (Wesendonk-Lieder)

New York April 1961	Taubman, piano	LP: RCA LM 2578/LSC 2578
London 1972	LSO C.Davis	LP: Philips 6500 294

Tristan und Isolde

Characters in order of appearance

YOUNG SEAMAN	ERMANNO MAURO
ISOLDE	BIRGIT NILSSON
BRANGÄNE	JOSEPHINE VEASEY
KURWENAL	DONALD McINTYRE
TRISTAN	JESS THOMAS
MELOT	JOHN DOBSON
KING MARK	DAVID WARD
SHEPHERD	JOHN LANIGAN
STEERSMAN	GWYNNE HOWELL

Sailors

Schoolgirls are from the Edith Cavell School and have been coached by Jean Povey

The Royal Opera House would like to express their thanks to Hawker Siddeley Aviation Ltd. for providing facilities for aerial photographs.

John Bury is a member of the Royal Shakespeare Company

Assistant to John Bury—Anna Steiner

Scenery painted by Peter Courtier
Scenery built by Tom Walker
Costumes made by Gabriella Mustillo and Sergio Piatto
Properties made by Andy Hall
Wigs made by Albert Sargood
Fabrics dyed and painted by Valerie Connell
Jewellery and head-dresses by Jean Percival
} COVENT GARDEN PRODUCTION DEPARTMENT

Scenery for Act II built and painted by Victor Mara Ltd.
Projection slides by Reg Wilson
Shoes by Anello & Davide
Programme photographs from the Harold Rosenthal Collection.

30 June 1971

Tuesday, 4th October, 1960

The 152nd performance at the Royal Opera House

of

Die Walküre

MUSIC DRAMA IN THREE ACTS

(being the first day of the Trilogy
"Der Ring des Nibelungen")

Words and music by Richard Wagner

Scenery and costumes by Leslie Hurry

Production rehearsed by Erich Witte

CONDUCTOR — RUDOLF KEMPE

THE COVENT GARDEN ORCHESTRA
Leader — Charles Taylor

This opera was first performed at the Royal Court Theatre, Munich, 26th June, 1870, with Sophie Stehle, Therese Vogl, Anna Kaufmann, Heinrich Vogl, August Kindermann, Herr Bausewein, conductor Franz Wüllner. It was first performed at Bayreuth in 1876; in London at Her Majesty's Theatre, 6th May, 1882, conductor Seidl; at Covent Garden on 29th June 1892, with Ende-Andriessen, Senger-Bettaque, Schumann-Heink, Alvary, Reichmann, Wiegand, conductor Mahler.

CHARACTERS IN ORDER OF APPEARANCE

SIEGMUND	WOLFGANG WINDGASSEN
SIEGLINDE	AMY SHUARD
HUNDING	DAVID WARD
WOTAN	HANS HOTTER
BRÜNNHILDE	BIRGIT NILSSON
FRICKA	URSULA BÖSE
VALKYRIES	
GERHILDE	ROSINA RAISBECK
ORTLINDE	UNA HALE
WALTRAUTE	MARGRETA ELKINS
SCHWERTLEITE	MONICA SINCLAIR
HELMWIGE	JUDITH PIERCE
SIEGRUNE	NOREEN BERRY
GRIMGERDE	HEATHER BEGG
ROSSWEISSE	JOSEPHINE VEASEY

DER RING DES NIBELUNGEN

A stage-festival play for three days and a preliminary evening (Ein Bühnenfestspiel für drei Tage und einem Vorabend), words and music by Richard Wagner.

The first performance of the entire Cycle took place at the Festspielhaus, Bayreuth on 13th, 14th, 16th and 17th August, 1876. Das Rheingold had been given on 22nd September, 1869, at the Royal Court Theatre, Munich, and Die Walküre at the same theatre on 26th June, 1870.

The first complete Cycle in London was given at Her Majesty's Theatre on 5th, 6th, 8th and 9th May, 1882, under An on Seidl and sung in German.

The first Cycle at Covent Garden took place in June, 1892, but the four operas were given in this order: Siegfried, Rheingold, Walküre, Götterdämmerung, so that the tenor, Max Alvary, could make his Covent Garden debut as the young Siegfried. This first complete ring in English was sung at Covent Garden under Hans Richter in January, 1908.

Weber

Der Freischütz

Munich 1968	Role of Agathe Köth, Gedda, Berry, Crass Bavarian State Chorus & Orchestra Heger	LP: EMI 1C 165 28351-28353 Excerpts LP: EMI 1C 063 29023

Der Freischütz: Excerpt (Leise, leise)

London May 1958	Philharmonia Wallberg	LP: Columbia 33CX 1629/SAX 2284 LP: Angel 35715/60353 LP: EMI 1C 187 00786-00787 CD: EMI CDM 763 1082/CD-CFP 4561
London June 1963	Covent Garden Orchestra Downes	LP: Decca LXT 6077/SXL 6077

Oberon

Munich March and December 1970	Role of Rezia Hamari, Domingo, Grobe, Prey Bavarian Radio Chorus & Orchestra Kubelik	LP: DG 2709 035/2726 052 CD: DG 419 0382 Excerpts LP: DG 2538 098/2721 206

Oberon: Excerpt (Ozean, du Ungeheuer)

London May 1958	Philharmonia Wallberg	LP: Columbia 33CX 1629/SAX 2284 LP: Angel 35715/60353 LP: EMI ASD 3915/1C 187 00786-00787 CD: EMI CDM 763 1082
Stockholm August 1961	Stockholm PO Grevillius	CD: Bluebell ABCD 055
London June 1963	Covent Garden Orchestra Downes	LP: Decca LXT 6077/SXL 6077

Wenneberg

Man borde inte sorva

Sweden   Roos, piano   LP: Bluebell BELL 114
1978-1979

Wiklund

Silkesko over gylden laest

New York   Wustman, piano   CD: Melodram MEL 18027
November 1967

Miscellaneous

I rosens doft

Stockholm   Oestman, piano   LP: Swedish Society SLT 33243
December 1975

The Golden Ring: TV film of the making of Decca's Solti Ring

Vienna   Watson, Windgassen, VHS Video: Decca 071 1533
1965   Fischer-Dieskau,   Laserdisc: Decca 071 1531
                Frick
                VPO
                Solti

Hinter den Kulissen der Gotterdammerung: German language version of the above

Vienna   Watson, Windgassen, VHS Video: Decca 071 0023
1965   Fischer-Dieskau,
                Frick
                VPO
                Solti

Gwyneth Jones
born 1936

Discography compiled by John Hunt

Introduction

The German musicologist Klaus Geitel has written an appreciation of Dame Gwyneth Jones in which he compares her arrival on the operatic scene in the 1960s to a refreshing sea wave off the coast of her Welsh homeland. Although the Welsh were always known for their singing, writes Geitel, Dame Gwyneth set out as if she were the first and as if she were not going to rest until she had become the best.

There was indeed a recklessness and high exuberance about those early days. It can be heard in her recorded Senta and Leonore, versions which did not endear themselves to lovers of the seamless line and of tonal purity. Here was the successor to Jeritza and Rysanek rather than to Seinemeyer and Rethberg, spanning the repertoires of German dramatic soprano and Italian spinto.

A cluster of major roles in recorded opera from 1969 until 1974, which appeared perhaps within too short a time of each other, were followed by a lull in studio work which has never really regained momentum. Invitations by major labels have been restricted to special cases of rare works, Strauss' Aegyptische Helena and Schmidt's Notre Dame among them. And yet the faith placed in the soprano (who, like Mödl before her, started out as a mezzo) by great maestri like Böhm and Kleiber is tribute indeed to her absolute musicality and absorption into the Central European opera tradition to an extent not common or easy for an Anglo-Saxon.

Gwyneth Jones has sung roles in all the main Wagner stage works, only Lohengrin being something of a stumbling block: there has been no Elsa (although a 1990 recording of "Einsam in trüben Tagen" illustrates how great our loss must be). Some amends are being made now, as she has begun to sing Ortrud on stage 20 years after performing the role in Deutsche Grammophon's studios. But this was a minor omission compared to the intensity she has applied to the rest of Wagner - and Strauss !
We have both Elisabeth and Venus (preserved in a remarkable video, in my view even more impressive than her video-recorded Brünnhilde), Sieglinde and Brünnhilde, Chrysothemis and Elektra, Oktavian and Marschallin, Empress and Färberin (in one and the same stage performance, believe it or not !). The list spills over into the Italian repertoire - Turandot, Tosca, Aida, Elisabetta, Minnie. It soon becomes clear that for a singer of such voracious artistic appetite - and a voice and heart to match - the visual element cannot be neglected, and why some attention must be paid in a discography to the unpublished video material.

As Leonard Bernstein once wrote to Dame Gwyneth Jones:
- G Glorious voice
- W Wonderful range
- Y Youthful ardour
- N Noble heart
- E Endless enthusiasm
- T Truth-loving artist
- H Heil Dir, Gwyneth !!

John Hunt

Beethoven

Fidelio

Dresden March 1969	Role of Leonore Mathis, Schreier, King, Talvela, Adam, Crass Dresden & Leipzig Opera Choruses Dresden Staatskapelle Böhm	LP: DG 2709 031/2720 113/2721 136 CD: DG 445 6752 Excerpts LP: DG 2537 002
Hamburg 1970	Role of Leonore Miljakovic, Grobe, King, Greindl, Neidlinger, Talvela Hamburg Opera Chorus Philharmonisches Staatsorchester Böhm	Unpublished video recording

Another performance may be preserved, as a Metropolitan opera broadcast with Jones in the role of Leonore took place in February 1976

Fidelio: Excerpt (Abscheulicher !)

Vienna March 1966	VPO Quadri	LP: Decca SXL 6249

Fidelio: Excerpt (Mir ist so wunderbar)

London 1967	Robson, Dobson, Kelly Covent Garden Orchestra Solti	LP: Decca SET 392-393

Symphony No 9 "Choral"

Vienna April 1970	<u>Soprano soloist</u> Troyanos, J.Thomas, Ridderbusch Vienna Opera Chorus VPO Böhm	LP: DG 2707 073/2720 045/2721 080 LP: DG 2721 154/2740 115/413 2211 CD: DG 427 1962
Salzburg August 1979	<u>Soprano soloist</u> H.Schwarz, Kollo, Moll Vienna Opera Chorus VPO Bernstein	LP: DG 2707 124/2740 216 CD: DG 410 8592/423 4812 VHS Video: DG 072 1083 Laserdisc: DG 072 1081

Ah perfido !

Vienna March 1966	VPO Quadri	LP: Decca SXL 6249

Britten

A War Requiem

Ottobeuren 1976	Soprano soloist Pears, Shirley-Quirk Bavarian Radio Chorus & Orchestra Kubelik	Unpublished video recording

Cherubini

Medea

Rome August 1967	Role of Medea Lorengar, Cossotto, Prevedi, Diaz Santa Cecilia Chorus & Orchestra Gardelli	LP: Decca SET 376-378

Medea: Excerpt (Dei tuoi figli)

Vienna March 1966	VPO Quadri	LP: Decca SXL 6249

Monday 11th July and Tuesday 12th July

NEW PHILHARMONIA ORCHESTRA

LEADER: HUGH BEAN

Conducted by

CARLO MARIA GIULINI

with

GWYNETH JONES *(Soprano)*

JOSEPHINE VEASEY *(Mezzo-Soprano)*

NICOLAI GEDDA *(Tenor)*

RAFAEL ARIE *(Bass)*

and

THE NEW PHILHARMONIA CHORUS

CHORUS MASTER: WILHELM PITZ

National Anthem	arranged by Britten
Requiem Mass	Verdi

ST. PAUL'S CATHEDRAL AT 8 P.M.

By permission of the Dean and Chapter

ERRATUM: National Anthem arranged by Britten will not now be played.

Wigmore Hall

Manager: William Lyne
Lessees: The Arts Council of Great Britain

Opening Concert of the 1986/87 Season
Thursday 11 September 1986 at 7.30 pm
Song Recital and Late Romantics Series

Dame Gwyneth Jones soprano
Geoffrey Parsons piano

PROGRAMME

Would patrons with digital watch alarms please ensure that they are switched off

Die junge Nonne (D828, 1825)   **Franz Schubert (1797-1828)**
Die Sterne (D684, 1828)
Auf dem Wasser zu singen (D774, 1823)
Du bist die Ruh (D776, 1823)
Gretchen am Spinnrade (D118, 1814)

Wesendonk Lieder (Fünf Gedichte für eine Frauenstimme, 1857-58)   **Richard Wagner (1813-1883)**
    Der Engel
    Stehe Still!
    Im Treibhaus
    Schmerzen
    Träume

====== Interval ======

Seven Early Songs (1905-08)   **Alban Berg (1885-1935)**
    Nacht
    Schilflied
    Die Nachtigall
    Traumgekrönt
    Im Zimmer
    Liebesode
    Sommertage

Ständchen (op 17 no 2, 1886)   **Richard Strauss (1864-1949)**
Morgen (op 27 no 4, 1894)
Wiegenlied (op 41 no 1, 1899)
Frühlingsfeier (op 56 no 5, 1904-06)

Humperdinck

Hänsel und Gretel

Dresden 1992	Role of Mother Gruberova, Murray, C.Ludwig, Grundheber Dresden Staatskapelle C.Davis	CD: Philips 438 0132

Hänsel und Gretel: Excerpts (Brüderchen, komm' tanz mit mir; Abends will ich schlafen geh'n)

Zürich 1963	Role of Hänsel Pfleger Zürich Opera Orchestra Mersson	LP: Concert Hall M 5020

James

Hen wlad fy nhadau (Land of my fathers), arranged Hannam

Cardiff May 1992	O'Neill, T.Jones, Sammons World Choir Bands of the Guards Division Hughes	CD: EMI CDC 754 6282

Lehar

Die lustige Witwe

Berlin December 1979	Role of Hanna Kollo, Jerusalem Deutsche Oper Chorus & Orchestra C.Richter	Unpublished video recording

Die lustige Witwe: Excerpt (Vilja-Lied)

Ebbw Vale March 1980	Dyfed Choir BBC Welsh SO C.Davis	Unpublished video recording
1985	Details of orchestra and conductor not confirmed	LP: CBS 24508

Lloyd Webber

Cats: Excerpt (Memory)

Verona August 1985	Polish State Philharmonic Orchestra Lloyd Webber	LP: Legendary LR 216 LP: Polygram 419 2801 CD: Polygram 419 2802

Mahler

Symphony No 8 "Symphony of a Thousand"

London April 1966	Soprano soloist Spoorenberg, Annear, Reynolds, Procter, Mitchinson, Rudzjack, McIntyre Leeds Festival Choir LSO Chorus LSO Bernstein	LP: CBS 77234 CD: Sony M3K 42199/SM3K 47551

Mascagni

Cavalleria Rusticana: Excerpt (Inneggiamo, il Signor non è morto)

Ebbw Vale March 1980	Dyfed Choir BBC Welsh SO C.Davis	Unpublished video recording

Mendelssohn

Elijah

London
July 1968

Soprano soloist
Baker, Gedda,
Fischer-Dieskau
New Philharmonia
Chorus & Orchestra
Frühbeck de Burgos

LP: EMI SLS 935

Monteverdi

L'Incoronazione di Poppea

Paris
March 1978

Role of Poppea
Masterson, C.Ludwig,
Vickers, Stilwell,
Ghiaurov
Paris Opéra
Chorus & Orchestra
Rudel

LP: Legendary LR 160
Also unpublished video recording

Poulenc

La voix humaine

Paris
May 1989

Orchestra
Baudo

Unpublished video recording

Puccini

Madama Butterfly: Excerpt (Un bel dì)

Pontypool April 1977	BBC Welsh SO Downes	LP: Legendary LR 210 Also unpublished video recording

La Fanciulla del West

Frankfurt 1992	Role of Minnie Murgu, Otelli Hungarian Radio Chorus Orchestra of Hessischer Rundfunk Viotti	CD: Sine Qua Non 398 20212

Tosca: Excerpt (Vissi d'arte)

Ebbw Vale March 1980	BBC Welsh SO C.Davis	Unpublished video recording
Location uncertain 1981	Orchestra Varviso	LP: Legendary LR 216

Turandot

London May 1987	Role of Turandot Haymon, Bonisolli, Lloyd Covent Garden Chorus & Orchestra Delacôte	Unpublished video recording

Turandot: Excerpts (In questa reggia; Straniero, ascolta)

Los Angeles July 1984	Domingo Covent Garden Chorus & Orchestra C.Davis	LP: Legendary LR 216

BAYERISCHE STAATSOPER
NATIONALTHEATER MÜNCHEN

16. April 1982

5. Abonnement-Vorstellung Freitag rot

MADAME BUTTERFLY

Tragödie einer Japanerin in drei Akten (nach J. L. Long und D. Belasco)
von L. Illica und G. Giacosa

Musik von
GIACOMO PUCCINI
In italienischer Sprache

Musikalische Leitung: Alexander Brezina
Inszenierung: Wolf Busse
Bühnenbild: Otto Stich · Kostüme: Silvia Strahammer
Choreinstudierung: Josef Beischer

PERSONEN

Cho-Cho-San, genannt Butterfly	Gwyneth Jones
Suzuki, Dienerin der Cho-Cho-San	Gudrun Wewezow
B. F. Pinkerton Leutnant in der Marine der USA	Corneliu Murgu
Kate Pinkerton	Helena Jungwirth
Sharpless, Konsul der Vereinigten Staaten in Nagasaki	Raimund Grumbach
Goro Nakodo	Friedrich Lenz
Der Fürst Yamadori	Georg Paskuda
Onkel Bonzo	Karl Helm
Yakusidé	Wilfried Michl
Der Kaiserliche Kommissär	Hermann Sapell
Der Standesbeamte	Gerhard Auer
Die Mutter der Cho-Cho-San	Monika Schmitt
Die Base	Carmen Anhorn
Die Tante	Angela Feeney
Das Kind	Stefanie Mösch

Ein japanischer Koch
Ein japanischer Diener
Verwandte, Freunde und Freundinnen von Cho-Cho-San
Gefolge des Onkel Bonzo

Das Bayerische Staatsorchester · Der Chor der Bayerischen Staatsoper

Abendspielleitung: Bijan Ahsef

Inspektion: Horst Wruck
und Herbert Gurth
Souffleuse: Ingrid von Eckardstein

Technische Gesamtleitung: Helmut Großer
Bühne: Josef Gebert
Beleuchtung: Johann Darchinger
Leiter des Kostümwesens: Günter Berger
Kostümgestaltung: Silvia Strahammer
Masken: Rudolf Herbert

Das Werk ist erschienen im Verlag G. Ricordi & Co., München.

Anfang 19.00 Uhr   Pause nach dem 1. Akt   Ende ca. 21.45 Uhr
Die sechste Abonnement-Vorstellung Freitag rot findet am 14. Mai statt.

Schmidt

Notre Dame

Berlin
August 1988

Role of Esmeralda
Borris, King,
Laubenthal, Moll,
Welker
Berlin Radio
Chorus & Orchestra
Prick

CD: Capriccio CD 10248-10249

Schoenberg

Erwartung

London
October 1990

BBC SO
A.Davis

Unpublished radio broadcast

Sibelius

Luonnotar

Wembley
February 1969

LSO
Dorati

LP: EMI ASD 2486
CD: EMI CDM 565 1822

Richard Strauss

Die Aegyptische Helena

Detroit May 1979	Role of Helena Hendricks, Finnilä, Kastu, White Jewell Chorale Detroit SO Dorati	LP: Decca D176 D3 CD: Decca 430 3812

Elektra

Orange July 1991	Role of Elektra Connell, Rysanek, King, Estes Orchestre National Janowski	Unpublished video recording Video extracts from a Geneva performance with Jones in the role of Elektra may also exist

Elektra: Excerpt (Weh! Ach ganz allein)

Berlin 1985	Deutsche Oper Orchestra Hollreiser	LP: Legendary LR 216

Die Frau ohne Schatten

Paris 1980	Role of Färberin Behrens, Dunn, Kollo, Berry, Grundheber Paris Opéra Chorus & Orchestra Dohnanyi	Unpublished video recording

Der Rosenkavalier

Vienna March and April 1971	Role of Oktavian C.Ludwig, Popp, Domingo, Berry, Gutstein Vienna Opera Chorus VPO Bernstein	LP: CBS 77416 CD: Sony M3K 42564
Munich July 1977	Role of Marschallin Popp, Fassbänder, Unger, Ridderbusch, Kusche Bavarian State Chorus & Orchestra C.Kleiber	LP: Legendary LR 179 CD: Legendary LRCD 1014
Munich May 1979	Role of Marschallin Popp, Fassbänder, Araiza, Jungwirth, Kusche Bavarian State Chorus & Orchestra C.Kleiber	VHS Video: DG 072 4053 Laserdisc: DG 072 4051

Another performance may be preserved, as a Metropolitan opera broadcast with Jones in the role of the Marschallin took place in January 1978

Salome

Hamburg November 1970	Role of Salome Dunn, Ochman, Cassilly, Fischer-Dieskau Philharmonisches Staatsorchester Böhm	LP: DG 2707 052/2721 186

Another performance may be preserved, as a Metropolitan opera broadcast with Jones in the role of Salome took place in March 1981

Salome: Excerpt (Closing scene)

Ebbw Vale March 1980	BBC Welsh SO C.Davis	Unpublished video recording

Frühling (4 letzte Lieder)

Tokyo
May 1991
Tokyo SO
Paternostro
CD: Koch Schwann 314.081

September (4 letzte Lieder)

Tokyo
May 1991
Tokyo SO
Paternostro
CD: Koch Schwann 314.081

Beim Schlafengehen (4 letzte Lieder)

Tokyo
May 1991
Tokyo SO
Paternostro
CD: Koch Schwann 314.081

Im Abendrot (4 letzte Lieder)

Tokyo
May 1991
Tokyo SO
Paternostro
CD: Koch Schwann 314.081

Allerseelen

Berlin
December 1988
Parsons, piano
CD: Capriccio 10 258

All' mein Gedanken

Berlin
December 1988
Parsons, piano
CD: Capriccio 10 258

Cäcilie

Berlin
December 1988
Parsons, piano
CD: Capriccio 10 258

Tokyo
May 1991
Tokyo SO
Paternostro
CD: Koch Schwann 314.081

Du meines Herzens Krönelein

Berlin
December 1988
Parsons, piano
CD: Capriccio 10 258

Freundliche Vision

Tokyo
May 1991
Tokyo SO
Paternostro
CD: Koch Schwann 314.081

Dienstag, 29. September 1992 **STAATSOPER**

97. Aufführung in dieser Inszenierung

Ariadne auf Naxos

Oper in einem Aufzug
nebst einem Vorspiel von   Hugo von Hofmannsthal

Musik   Richard Strauss

Dirigent   Ulf Schirmer
Inszenierung und Ausstattung   Filippo Sanjust

Personen des Vorspiels
Der Haushofmeister   Helmut Lohner
Der Musiklehrer   Peter Weber
Der Komponist   Jeanne Piland
Der Tenor (Bacchus)   Michael Pabst
Ein Offizier   Anton Wendler
Ein Tanzmeister   Heinz Zednik
Ein Perückenmacher   Jörg Schneider
Ein Lakai   Alfred Šramek
Zerbinetta   Barbara Kilduff
Primadonna (Ariadne)   Gwyneth Jones
Harlekin   Wolfgang Glashof
Scaramuccio   Franz Kasemann
Truffaldin   Roland Schubert
Brighella   Herwig Pecoraro

Personen der Oper
Ariadne   Gwyneth Jones
Bacchus   Michael Pabst
Najade   Yelda Kodalli
Dryade   Waltraud Winsauer
Echo   Joanna Borowska
Zerbinetta   Barbara Kilduff
Harlekin   Wolfgang Glashof
Scaramuccio   Franz Kasemann
Truffaldin   Roland Schubert
Brighella   Herwig Pecoraro

Salome

Characters in order of appearance

NARRABOTH, a young Syrian, Captain of the Guard	ADRIAN DE PEYER
PAGE TO HERODIAS	GILLIAN KNIGHT
FIRST SOLDIER	PAUL HUDSON
SECOND SOLDIER	MICHAEL LANGDON
JOKANAAN (John the Baptist)	NORMAN BAILEY
A CAPPADOCIAN	PAUL STATHAM
SALOME, daughter of Herodias	GWYNETH JONES
A SLAVE	RUTH GURNER
HEROD, King of Judea	RAGNAR ULFUNG
HERODIAS, wife of Herod	HEATHER BEGG
FIRST JEW	FRANCIS EGERTON
SECOND JEW	ROBERT THOMAS
THIRD JEW	JOHN DOBSON
FOURTH JEW	RICHARD GREAGER
FIFTH JEW	DENNIS WICKS
FIRST NAZARENE	RICHARD VAN ALLAN
SECOND NAZARENE	WILLIAM ELVIN

Dennis Wicks is a member of Sadler's Wells Opera Company

Salome's dance choreographed by Romayne Grigorova

6 April 1974

Frühlingsfeier

Berlin   Parsons, piano   CD: Capriccio 10 258
December 1988

Tokyo   Tokyo   CD: Koch Schwann 314.081
May 1991   Paternostro

Die heiligen 3 Könige aus Morgenland

Tokyo   Tokyo SO   CD: Koch Schwann 314.081
May 1991   Paternostro

Heimliche Aufforderung

Berlin   Parsons, piano   CD: Capriccio 10 258
December 1988

In goldener Fülle

Berlin   Parsons, piano   CD: Capriccio 10 258
December 1988

Mit deinen blauen Augen

Berlin   Parsons, piano   CD: Capriccio 10 258
December 1988

Morgen

Berlin   Parsons, piano   CD: Capriccio 10 258
December 1988

Tokyo   Tokyo SO   CD: Koch Schwann 314.081
May 1991

Die Nacht

Berlin   Parsons, piano   CD: Capriccio 10 258
December 1988

Nachtgesang

Berlin   Parsons, piano   CD: Capriccio 10 258
December 1988

Ruhe, meine Seele

Berlin Parsons, piano CD: Capriccio 10 258
December 1988

Tokyo Tokyo SO CD: Koch Schwann 314.081
May 1991 Paternostro

Schlagende Herzen

Berlin Parsons, piano CD: Capriccio 10 258
December 1988

Schlechtes Wetter

Berlin Parsons, piano CD: Capriccio 10 258
December 1988

Ständchen

Berlin Parsons, piano CD: Capriccio 10 258
December 1988

Traum durch die Dämmerung

Berlin Parsons, piano CD: Capriccio 10 258
December 1988

Wiegenlied

Berlin Parsons, piano CD: Capriccio 10 258
December 1988

Tokyo Tokyo SO CD: Koch Schwann 314.081
May 1991 Paternostro

Die Zeitlose

Berlin Parsons, piano CD: Capriccio 10 258
December 1988

Zueignung

Berlin Parsons, piano CD: Capriccio 10 258
December 1988

Tokyo Tokyo SO CD: Koch Schwann 314/081
May 1991 Paternostro

The 378th performance at the Royal Opera House of

Aida

Opera in 4 acts

Scenario by Auguste Mariette
Text by Camille du Locle translated into Italian verse by Antonio Ghislanzoni
Music by GIUSEPPE VERDI
(Property of G. Ricordi & Co.)

Conductor EDWARD DOWNES
Producer PETER POTTER
Scenery and costumes NICHOLAS GEORGIADIS
Choreographer PETER WRIGHT
Lighting WILLIAM BUNDY

THE COVENT GARDEN OPERA CHORUS
Chorus Master Douglas Robinson

THE COVENT GARDEN ORCHESTRA
Leader Charles Taylor

Characters in order of appearance

RAMFIS, *High Priest of Isis*	JOSEPH ROULEAU
RADAMES, *Captain of the Egyptian Guard*	JON VICKERS
AMNERIS, *daughter of the King of Egypt*	CHRISTA LUDWIG
AIDA, *Ethiopian slave to Amneris*	GWYNETH JONES
THE KING OF EGYPT	DENNIS WICKS
A MESSENGER	GLYNNE THOMAS
A PRIESTESS	ANNE FINLEY
AMONASRO, *King of Ethiopia, father of Aida*	JOHN SHAW
SOLO DANCERS	MONICA MASON DAVID DREW IAN HAMILTON PETER O'BRIEN

Ministers of the King, Priests and Priestesses, Officers and Soldiers, Attendants on Amneris, People of Egypt, Ethiopian Prisoners.

THE COVENT GARDEN OPERA BALLET
Ballet Mistress Romayne Grigorova

30 January 1968

Royal Opera House Covent Garden Limited
General Administrator JOHN TOOLEY

in association with

Scott Concert Promotions Limited

presents

GWYNETH JONES
Soprano

GEOFFREY PARSONS
Piano

Sunday 7 May 1978

The Royal Opera House Covent Garden Limited receives financial assistance from The Arts Council of Great Britain

In accordance with the requirements of the Greater London Council: persons shall not be permitted to stand or sit in any of the gangways intersecting the seating, or to sit in any of the other gangways; smoking and the taking of photographs in the auditorium are not permitted.

Verdi

Aida

London January 1968	Role of Aida Dourian, Vickers, Shaw, Rouleau Covent Garden Chorus & Orchestra Downes	CD: Melodram CDM 27019
London September 1968	Role of Aida Bumbry, Craig, Shaw, Rouleau Covent Garden Chorus & Orchestra Downes	Unpublished video recording

Aida: Excerpt (Ritorna vincitor)

London January and February 1968	Covent Garden Orchestra Downes	LP: Decca SXL 6376/414 4421
Pontypool April 1977	BBC Welsh SO Downes	Unpublished video recording

Aida: Excerpt (O patria mia)

London January and February 1968	Covent Garden Orchestra Downes	LP: Decca SXL 6376/414 4421

Don Carlo: Excerpts (La regina!..Una canzon qui lieta risuonò; Giustizia, o Sire!..Ciel! Che mai feci)

Vienna May 1967	Role of Elisabetta C.Ludwig, Paskalis, Ghiaurov VPO Klobucar	CD: Melodram MEL 26516

'Don Carlo: Excerpt (Tu che la vanità)

London January and February 1968	Covent Garden Orchestra Downes	LP: Decca SXL 6376/414 4421

A performance of Don Carlo was presented for Japanese TV in 1972, with Jones in the role of Elisabetta and with Sesto Bruscantini also in the cast; this may eventually appear in video format

La Forza del destino: Excerpt (Pace, pace, mio Dio!)

Vienna March 1966	VPO Quadri	LP: Decca SXL 6249
Ebbw Vale March 1980	BBC Welsh SO C.Davis	Unpublished video recording

Macbeth

Tokyo March 1992	Role of Lady Macbeth Cupido, Bruson, Scandiuzzi Tokyo Chorus Tokyo PO Kuhn	CD: Sine Qua Non 398 20242

Macbeth: Excerpt (Vieni! T'affretta/Or tutti, sorgete)

London January and February 1968	Macpherson Covent Garden Orchestra Downes	LP: Decca SXL 6376/414 4421
Pontypool April 1977	BBC Welsh SO Downes	Unpublished video recording
Location uncertain 1982	Orchestra Masini	LP: Legendary LR 216

Otello

Walthamstow August and October 1968	Role of Desdemona Di Stasio, McCracken, Fischer-Dieskau Ambrosian Singers New Philharmonia Orchestra Barbirolli	LP: EMI SLS 940 LP: Angel 3742 LP: EMI EX 29 01373

Otello: Excerpt (Piangea cantando....Ave Maria)

London January and February 1968	Lehane Covent Garden Orchestra Downes	LP: Decca SXL 6376/414 4421

Il Trovatore

London November 1964	Role of Leonora Simionato, Prevedi, Glossop, Rouleau Covent Garden Chorus & Orchestra Giulini	LP: Legendary LR 175

Il Trovatore: Excerpt (D'amor sull' ali rosee)

Vienna March 1966	VPO Quadri	LP: Decca SXL 6249

Requiem

USA 1967	Soprano soloist Bumbry, Corelli, Flagello Unidentified Chorus & Orchestra Mehta	LP: Legendary LR 125 Some confusion surrounds this unofficial issue; it could be from Los Angeles, Dallas or Chicago

Wagner

Der fliegende Holländer

Bayreuth July 1971	Role of Senta S.Wagner, Esser, Ek, Stewart, Ridderbusch Bayreuth Festival Chorus & Orchestra Böhm	LP: DG 2709 040/2720 052 LP: DG 2740 140/413 2911 CD: DG 437 7102 Excerpts LP: DG 2537 024
London 1975	Role of Senta Bailey, Dean Orchestra & Chorus Lloyd-Jones	Unpublished video recording

Der fliegende Holländer: Excerpt (Traft ihr das Schiff im Meere an)

Vienna March 1966	Vienna Opera Chorus VPO Quadri	LP: Decca SXL 6249

Götterdämmerung

Vienna October and November 1964	Role of Wellgunde Nilsson, Watson, C.Ludwig, Windgassen, Fischer-Dieskau, Frick, Neidlinger Vienna Opera Chorus VPO Solti	LP: Decca MET 292-297/SET 292-297 LP: Decca D100 D19/RING 1-22 LP: Decca 414 1001/414 1151 CD: Decca 414 1002/414 1152

Bayreuth
August 1980
	Role of Brünnhilde
	Altmeyer, Killebrew,
	Jung, Mazura,
	Becht, Hübner
	Bayreuth Festival
	Chorus & Orchestra
	Boulez
		LP: Philips 6769 073/6769 074
		CD: Philips 434 4242/434 4202
		VHS Video: Philips
		   070 4043/070 4073/070 4303
		Laserdisc: Philips
		   070 4041/070 4301
		Excerpts
		CD: Philips 426 2112

Another performance may be preserved, as a Metropolitan opera broadcast with Jones in the role of Brünnhilde took place in March 1993

Götterdämmerung: Excerpt (Starke Scheite schichtet mir dort)

Pontypool April 1977	BBC Welsh SO Downes	Unpublished video recording
Cologne August 1990	WDR Orchestra Paternostro	CD: Chandos CHAN 8930

Lohengrin

Munich 1971	Role of Ortrud Janowitz, King, Stewart, Nienstedt, Ridderbusch Bavarian Radio Chorus & Orchestra Kubelik	LP: DG 2713 005/2720 036/2740 141 CD: DG (Japan) POCG 2874-2876 Excerpts LP: DG 2537 026

Lohengrin: Excerpt (Einsam in trüben Tagen)

Cologne August 1990	WDR Orchestra Paternostro	CD: Chandos CHAN 8930

Parsifal

Bayreuth July and August 1970	Role of Kundry King, Crass, Stewart, McIntyre, Ridderbusch Bayreuth Festival Chorus & Orchestra Boulez	LP: DG 2713 004/2720 034/2740 143 CD: DG 435 7182 Excerpts LP: DG 2537 025

Siegfried

Bayreuth
August 1979
	Role of Brünnhilde
	Sharp, Wenkel,
	Jung, Zednik, Becht,
	McIntyre, Hübner
	Bayreuth Festival
	Orchestra
	Boulez
		LP: Philips 6769 072/6769 074
		CD: Philips 434 4232/434 4202
		VHS Video: Philips
		   070 4033/070 4073/070 4303
		Laserdisc: Philips
		   070 4031/070 4301

Another performance may be preserved, as a Metropolitan opera broadcast with Jones in the role of Brünnhilde took place in March 1993

Thursday, 12th September, 1968

The 170th performance at the Royal Opera House of

Die Walküre

Music drama in three acts
(being the first day of the Trilogy "Der Ring des Nibelungen")

Words and music by RICHARD WAGNER

Conductor GEORG SOLTI

Originally produced by HANS HOTTER
Rehearsed by PETER POTTER

Scenery and costumes by
GÜNTHER SCHNEIDER-SIEMSSEN

Lighting by WILLIAM BUNDY and
GÜNTHER SCHNEIDER-SIEMSSEN

THE COVENT GARDEN ORCHESTRA
Leader Charles Taylor

Die Walküre

Characters in order of appearance

SIEGMUND	JAMES KING
SIEGLINDE	GWYNETH JONES
HUNDING	MICHAEL LANGDON
WOTAN	THEO ADAM
BRÜNNHILDE	AMY SHUARD
FRICKA	JOSEPHINE VEASEY
GERHILDE	AVA JUNE
ORTLINDE	MARGARET KINGSLEY
WALTRAUTE	YVONNE MINTON
SCHWERTLEITE	ELIZABETH BAINBRIDGE
HELMWIGE	VIVIEN TOWNLEY
SIEGRUNE	NOREEN BERRY
GRIMGERDE	PATRICIA PURCELL
ROSSWEISSE	HEATHER BEGG

Margaret Kingsley appears by kind permission of Sadler's Wells Opera Company

The Royal Opera House
General Director Sir John Tooley

The Royal Opera

presents

Tannhäuser
und der Sängerkrieg auf dem Wartburg

Music Director Sir Colin Davis

Opera in three acts

Music and poem Richard Wagner

Producer Elijah Moshinsky
Scenery Timothy O'Brien
Costumes Luciana Arrighi
Lighting Nick Chelton
Choreographer Kenneth MacMillan

Conductor Colin Davis

Tannhäuser

Characters in order of appearance

Tannhäuser	Klaus König 25, 28 September, 1 & 4 October
	Spas Wenkoff 8, 13, 17 & 20 October
Venus	Eva Randová
A Shepherd Boy	Nicholas Sillitoe
Hermann *Landgraf von Thüringen*	Fritz Hübner
Walther von der Vogelweide	Horst Laubenthal
Heinrich der Schreiber	Kim Begley
Reinmar von Zweter	Roderick Earle
Bierolf	John Gibbs
Wolfram von Eschenbach	Thomas Allen
Elisabeth *niece of Landgraf Hermann*	Gwyneth Jones

Thuringian Nobles, Knights, Ladies, Elder and Younger Pilgrims, Noble Pages

Dancers
Linda Gibbs   Kate Harrison   Christopher Bannerman   Ross McKinnn

Assistants to the producer Kate Brown, Stephen Lawless
Chief répétiteur Gareth Morrell
German language coach Hilde Beal
Choreologist Malin Thoors

1 October 1984

Tannhäuser

Bayreuth August 1978	<u>Roles of Elisabeth and Venus</u> Wenkoff, Schunk, Weikl, Sotin Bayreuth Festival Chorus & Orchestra C.Davis	VHS Video: Philips 070 4123 Laserdisc: Philips 070 4121

Tannhäuser: Excerpt (Dich teure Halle)

Pontypool April 1977	BBC Welsh SO Downes	Unpublished video recording
Ebbw Vale March 1980	BBC Welsh SO C.Davis	Unpublished video recording
Cologne August 1990	WDR Orchestra Paternostro	CD: Chandos CHAN 8930

Tannhäuser: Excerpt (Allmächtige Jungfrau)

Cologne August 1990	WDR Orchestra Paternostro	CD: Chandos CHAN 8930

Tristan und Isolde

Brussels 1980s	Role of Isolde Budai, Wenkoff, Grundheber Monnaie Orchestra and Chorus Cambreling	Unpublished video recording
Paris February 1985	Role of Isolde Meier, Johns, Welker, Vogel Paris Opéra Chorus & Orchestra Janowski	Unpublished video recording

Another performance may be preserved, as a Metropolitan opera broadcast with Jones in the role of Isolde took place in January 1981

Tristan und Isolde: Excerpt (Mild und leise)

San Francisco November 1980	San Francisco Opera Orchestra Adler	LP: Legendary LR 216
Cologne August 1990	WDR Orchestra Paternostro	CD: Chandos CHAN 8930

Die Walküre

Bayreuth
August 1979
	Role of Brünnhilde
	Altmeyer, H.Schwarz,
	Hofmann, McIntyre,
	Salminen
	Bayreuth Festival
	Orchestra
	Boulez
		LP: Philips 6769 071/6769 074
		CD: Philips 434 4222/434 4202
		VHS Video: Philips
		    070 4023/070 4073/070 4303
		Laserdisc: Philips
		    070 4021/070 4301

Other performances may be preserved, as Metropolitan opera broadcasts with Jones in the role of Sieglinde took place in December 1972 and in the role of Brünnhilde in April 1983 and March 1993

Traditional

Battle Hymn of the Republic, arranged Walker

Cardiff May 1992	O'Neill, T.Jones World Choir Bands of the Guards Divisions Hughes	CD: EMI CDC 754 6282

Miscellaneous

The Making of the Chereau/Boulez Ring Bayreuth 1976-1980: TV documentary

Bayreuth 1976-1980	McIntyre, Chereau, Boulez, Large, F.Wagner, W.Wagner and others	VHS Video: Philips 070 4023 Laserdisc: Philips 070 4011

Wagner: A film by Tony Palmer

1982	Hofmann, Redgrave, Burton and others	Unpublished video recording

The Royal Opera House
General Director Sir John Tooley

presents

The Royal Opera

Music Director Bernard Haitink KBE

Elektra

Tragedy in one act by

Hugo von Hofmannsthal

Music **Richard Strauss**
(By arrangement with Boosey & Hawkes Music Publishers Limited)

Production **Rudolf Hartmann**
Design **Isabel Lambert**
Costumes realized by **Gillian Dixon**

Conductor **Gerd Albrecht**

Elektra

Characters in order of appearance

First Maid		Elizabeth Bainbridge
Second Maid		Karen Shelby
Third Maid		Gillian Knight
Fourth Maid		Angela Bostock
Fifth Maid		Judith Howarth
The Overseer		Elizabeth Vaughan
Elektra		Gwyneth Jones
Chrysothemis *her sister*		Ruth Falcon
Klytemnestra *their mother*		Helga Dernesch
Orest *brother of Elektra and Chrysothemis*		Willard White except 2 July Harald Stamm 2 July
Orest's Tutor		Geoffrey Moses
Aegisth		Kenneth Woollam
Servants of the Household		
An Old Servant		William Mackie
A Young Servant		Robin Leggate
The Trainbearer		Valerie Robinson
The Confidante		Patricia Purcell

Chief répétiteur Christopher McManus
German language coach Hilde Beal
English surtitles prepared by Peter Bloor
Scenery, costumes, props, jewellery, millinery, dyeing and wigs Royal Opera House Production Department
Surtitles manufactured by G & T Ltd

Surtitles sponsored by The Durrington Corporation

Credits

Valuable help with information for the preparation of "Giants of the keyboard" and "Six Wagnerian sopranos" came from :

Jonathan Brown, Paris
Dennis Brownbill, Bex
Clifford Elkin, Glasgow
Allan Evans, Flushing NY
Mathias Erhard, Berlin
Michael Gray, Alexandria VA
Syd Gray, Hove
Ken Jagger (EMI Classics), London
Gerald Kingsley, London
Roderick Krüsemann, Amsterdam
Yvonne Lakeram (Decca Records), London
Kevork Marouchian, Munich
Bruce Morrison, Gillingham
Alan Newcombe (DG), Hamburg
John Owen, London
Brian Pinder, Halifax
John Raymon, London
Seiichi Semba, Ehime
Roger Smithson, London
Neville Sumpter, Northolt
Terje Thorp, Oslo
Malcolm Walker, Harrow

Discographies by Travis & Emery:
Discographies by John Hunt.

1987: 978-1-906857-14-1: From Adam to Webern: the Recordings of von Karajan.

1991: 978-0-951026-83-0: 3 Italian Conductors and 7 Viennese Sopranos: 10 Discographies: Arturo Toscanini, Guido Cantelli, Carlo Maria Giulini, Elisabeth Schwarzkopf, Irmgard Seefried, Elisabeth Gruemmer, Sena Jurinac, Hilde Gueden, Lisa Della Casa, Rita Streich.

1992: 978-0-951026-85-4: Mid-Century Conductors and More Viennese Singers: 10 Discographies: Karl Boehm, Victor De Sabata, Hans Knappertsbusch, Tullio Serafin, Clemens Krauss, Anton Dermota, Leonie Rysanek, Eberhard Waechter, Maria Reining, Erich Kunz.

1993: 978-0-951026-87-8: More 20th Century Conductors: 7 Discographies: Eugen Jochum, Ferenc Fricsay, Carl Schuricht, Felix Weingartner, Josef Krips, Otto Klemperer, Erich Kleiber.

1994: 978-0-951026-88-5: Giants of the Keyboard: 6 Discographies: Wilhelm Kempff, Walter Gieseking, Edwin Fischer, Clara Haskil, Wilhelm Backhaus, Artur Schnabel.

1994: 978-0-951026-89-2: Six Wagnerian Sopranos: 6 Discographies: Frieda Leider, Kirsten Flagstad, Astrid Varnay, Martha Moedl, Birgit Nilsson, Gwyneth Jones.

1995: 978-0-952582-70-0: Musical Knights: 6 Discographies: Henry Wood, Thomas Beecham, Adrian Boult, John Barbirolli, Reginald Goodall, Malcolm Sargent.

1995: 978-0-952582-71-7: A Notable Quartet: 4 Discographies: Gundula Janowitz, Christa Ludwig, Nicolai Gedda, Dietrich Fischer-Dieskau.

1996: 978-0-952582-72-4: The Post-War German Tradition: 5 Discographies: Rudolf Kempe, Joseph Keilberth, Wolfgang Sawallisch, Rafael Kubelik, Andre Cluytens.

1996: 978-0-952582-73-1: Teachers and Pupils: 7 Discographies: Elisabeth Schwarzkopf, Maria Ivoguen, Maria Cebotari, Meta Seinemeyer, Ljuba Welitsch, Rita Streich, Erna Berger.

1996: 978-0-952582-77-9: Tenors in a Lyric Tradition: 3 Discographies: Peter Anders, Walther Ludwig, Fritz Wunderlich.

1997: 978-0-952582-78-6: The Lyric Baritone: 5 Discographies: Hans Reinmar, Gerhard Huesch, Josef Metternich, Hermann Uhde, Eberhard Waechter.

1997: 978-0-952582-79-3: Hungarians in Exile: 3 Discographies: Fritz Reiner, Antal Dorati, George Szell.

1997: 978-1-901395-00-6: The Art of the Diva: 3 Discographies: Claudia Muzio, Maria Callas, Magda Olivero.

1997: 978-1-901395-01-3: Metropolitan Sopranos: 4 Discographies: Rosa Ponselle, Eleanor Steber, Zinka Milanov, Leontyne Price.

1997: 978-1-901395-02-0: Back From The Shadows: 4 Discographies: Willem Mengelberg, Dimitri Mitropoulos, Hermann Abendroth, Eduard Van Beinum.

1997: 978-1-901395-03-7: More Musical Knights: 4 Discographies: Hamilton Harty, Charles Mackerras, Simon Rattle, John Pritchard.

1998: 978-1-901395-94-5: Conductors On The Yellow Label: 8 Discographies: Fritz Lehmann, Ferdinand Leitner, Ferenc Fricsay, Eugen Jochum, Leopold Ludwig, Artur Rother, Franz Konwitschny, Igor Markevitch.

1998: 978-1-901395-95-2: More Giants of the Keyboard: 5 Discographies: Claudio Arrau, Gyorgy Cziffra, Vladimir Horowitz, Dinu Lipatti, Artur Rubinstein.

1998: 978-1-901395-96-9: Mezzo and Contraltos: 5 Discographies: Janet Baker, Margarete Klose, Kathleen Ferrier, Giulietta Simionato, Elisabeth Hoengen.

1999: 978-1-901395-97-6: The Furtwaengler Sound Sixth Edition: Discography and Concert Listing.
1999: 978-1-901395-98-3: The Great Dictators: 3 Discographies: Evgeny Mravinsky, Artur Rodzinski, Sergiu Celibidache.
1999: 978-1-901395-99-0: Sviatoslav Richter: Pianist of the Century: Discography.
2000: 978-1-901395-04-4: Philharmonic Autocrat 1: Discography of: Herbert Von Karajan [Third Edition].
2000: 978-1-901395-05-1: Wiener Philharmoniker 1 - Vienna Philharmonic and Vienna State Opera Orchestras: Discography Part 1 1905-1954.
2000: 978-1-901395-06-8: Wiener Philharmoniker 2 - Vienna Philharmonic and Vienna State Opera Orchestras: Discography Part 2 1954-1989.
2001: 978-1-901395-07-5: Gramophone Stalwarts: 3 Separate Discographies: Bruno Walter, Erich Leinsdorf, Georg Solti.
2001: 978-1-901395-08-2: Singers of the Third Reich: 5 Discographies: Helge Roswaenge, Tiana Lemnitz, Franz Voelker, Maria Mueller, Max Lorenz.
2001: 978-1-901395-09-9: Philharmonic Autocrat 2: Concert Register of Herbert Von Karajan Second Edition.
2002: 978-1-901395-10-5: Sächsische Staatskapelle Dresden: Complete Discography.
2002: 978-1-901395-11-2: Carlo Maria Giulini: Discography and Concert Register.
2002: 978-1-901395-12-9: Pianists For The Connoisseur: 6 Discographies: Arturo Benedetti Michelangeli, Alfred Cortot, Alexis Weissenberg, Clifford Curzon, Solomon, Elly Ney.
2003: 978-1-901395-14-3: Singers on the Yellow Label: 7 Discographies: Maria Stader, Elfriede Troetschel, Annelies Kupper, Wolfgang Windgassen, Ernst Haefliger, Josef Greindl, Kim Borg.
2003: 978-1-901395-15-0: A Gallic Trio: 3 Discographies: Charles Muench, Paul Paray, Pierre Monteux.
2004: 978-1-901395-16-7: Antal Dorati 1906-1988: Discography and Concert Register.
2004: 978-1-901395-17-4: Columbia 33CX Label Discography.
2004: 978-1-901395-18-1: Great Violinists: 3 Discographies: David Oistrakh, Wolfgang Schneiderhan, Arthur Grumiaux.
2006: 978-1-901395-19-8: Leopold Stokowski: Second Edition of the Discography.
2006: 978-1-901395-20-4: Wagner Im Festspielhaus: Discography of the Bayreuth Festival.
2006: 978-1-901395-21-1: Her Master's Voice: Concert Register and Discography of Dame Elisabeth Schwarzkopf [Third Edition].
2007: 978-1-901395-22-8: Hans Knappertsbusch: Kna: Concert Register and Discography of Hans Knappertsbusch, 1888-1965. Second Edition.
2008: 978-1-901395-23-5: Philips Minigroove: Second Extended Version of the European Discography.
2009: 978-1-901395--24-2: American Classics: The Discographies of Leonard Bernstein and Eugene Ormandy.

Discography by Stephen J. Pettitt, edited by John Hunt:
1987: 978-1-906857-16-5: Philharmonia Orchestra: Complete Discography 1945-1987

Available from: Travis & Emery at 17 Cecil Court, London, UK. (+44) 20 7 240 2129. email on sales@travis-and-emery.com .

© Travis & Emery 2009

Music and Books published by Travis & Emery Music Bookshop:

Anon.: Hymnarium Sarisburiense, cum Rubricis et Notis Musicis.
Agricola, Johann Friedrich from Tosi: Anleitung zur Singkunst.
Bach, C.P.E.: edited W. Emery: Nekrolog or Obituary Notice of J.S. Bach.
Bateson, Naomi Judith: Alcock of Salisbury
Bathe, William: A Briefe Introduction to the Skill of Song
Bax, Arnold: Symphony #5, Arranged for Piano Four Hands by Walter Emery
Burney, Charles: The Present State of Music in France and Italy
Burney, Charles: The Present State of Music in Germany, The Netherlands ...
Burney, Charles: An Account of the Musical Performances ... Handel
Burney, Karl: Nachricht von Georg Friedrich Handel's Lebensumstanden.
Cobbett, W.W.: Cobbett's Cyclopedic Survey of Chamber Music. (2 vols.)
Corrette, Michel: Le Maitre de Clavecin
Crimp, Bryan: Dear Mr. Rosenthal ... Dear Mr. Gaisberg ...
Crimp, Bryan: Solo: The Biography of Solomon
d'Indy, Vincent: Beethoven: Biographie Critique
d'Indy, Vincent: Beethoven: A Critical Biography
d'Indy, Vincent: César Franck (in French)
Frescobaldi, Girolamo: D'Arie Musicali per Cantarsi. Primo & Secondo Libro.
Geminiani, Francesco: The Art of Playing the Violin.
Handel; Purcell; Boyce; Geene et al: Calliope or English Harmony: Volume First.
Hawkins, John: A General History of the Science and Practice of Music (5 vols.)
Herbert-Caesari, Edgar: The Science and Sensations of Vocal Tone
Herbert-Caesari, Edgar: Vocal Truth
Hopkins and Rimboult: The Organ. Its History and Construction.
Hunt, John: Adam to Webern: the recordings of von Karajan
Isaacs, Lewis: Hänsel and Gretel. A Guide to Humperdinck's Opera.
Isaacs, Lewis: Königskinder (Royal Children) A Guide to Humperdinck's Opera.
Lacassagne, M. l'Abbé Joseph : Traité Général des élémens du Chant.
Lascelles (née Catley), Anne: The Life of Miss Anne Catley.
Mainwaring, John: Memoirs of the Life of the Late George Frederic Handel
Malcolm, Alexander: A Treaty of Music: Speculative, Practical and Historical
Marx, Adolph Bernhard: Die Kunst des Gesanges, Theoretisch-Practisch
May, Florence: The Life of Brahms
Mellers, Wilfrid: Angels of the Night: Popular Female Singers of Our Time
Mellers, Wilfrid: Bach and the Dance of God
Mellers, Wilfrid: Beethoven and the Voice of God

Travis & Emery Music Bookshop
17 Cecil Court, London, WC2N 4EZ, United Kingdom.
Tel. (+44) 20 7240 2129

Music and Books published by Travis & Emery Music Bookshop:
Mellers, Wilfrid: Caliban Reborn - Renewal in Twentieth Century Music
Mellers, Wilfrid: François Couperin and the French Classical Tradition
Mellers, Wilfrid: Harmonious Meeting
Mellers, Wilfrid: Le Jardin Retrouvé, The Music of Frederic Mompou
Mellers, Wilfrid: Music and Society, England and the European Tradition
Mellers, Wilfrid: Music in a New Found Land: ... ... American Music
Mellers, Wilfrid: Romanticism and the Twentieth Century (from 1800)
Mellers, Wilfrid: The Masks of Orpheus: ...... the Story of European Music.
Mellers, Wilfrid: The Sonata Principle (from c. 1750)
Mellers, Wilfrid: Vaughan Williams and the Vision of Albion
Panchianio, Cattuffio: Rutzvanscad Il Giovine
Pearce, Charles: Sims Reeves, Fifty Years of Music in England.
Playford, John: An Introduction to the Skill of Musick.
Purcell, Henry et al: Harmonia Sacra ... The First Book, (1726)
Purcell, Henry et al: Harmonia Sacra ... Book II (1726)
Quantz, Johann: Versuch einer Anweisung die Flöte traversiere zu spielen.
Rameau, Jean-Philippe: Code de Musique Pratique, ou Methodes.
Rastall, Richard: The Notation of Western Music.
Rimbault, Edward: The Pianoforte, Its Origins, Progress, and Construction.
Rousseau, Jean Jacques: Dictionnaire de Musique
Rubinstein, Anton : Guide to the proper use of the Pianoforte Pedals.
Sainsbury, John S.: Dictionary of Musicians. Vol. I. (1825). 2 vols.
Simpson, Christopher: A Compendium of Practical Musick in Five Parts
Spohr, Louis: Autobiography
Spohr, Louis: Grand Violin School
Tans'ur, William: A New Musical Grammar; or The Harmonical Spectator
Terry, Charles Sanford: Four-Part Chorals of J.S. Bach. (German & English)
Terry, Charles Sanford: Joh. Seb. Bach, Cantata Texts, Sacred and Secular.
Terry, Charles Sanford: The Origins of the Family of Bach Musicians.
Tosi, Pierfrancesco: Opinioni de' Cantori Antichi, e Moderni
Van der Straeten, Edmund: History of the Violoncello, The Viol da Gamba ...
Van der Straeten, Edmund: History of the Violin, Its Ancestors... (2 vols.)
Walther, J. G.: Musicalisches Lexikon ober Musicalische Bibliothec

Travis & Emery Music Bookshop
17 Cecil Court, London, WC2N 4EZ, United Kingdom.
Tel. (+44) 20 7240 2129

© Travis & Emery 2009

www.ingramcontent.com/pod-product-compliance
Lightning Source LLC
Chambersburg PA
CBHW070938230426
43666CB00011B/2483